MR. AND MRS. DOG

Mr. and Mrs.

DOG

Our Travels, Trials, Adventures, and Epiphanies

Donald McCaig

UNIVERSITY OF VIRGINIA PRESS

CHARLOTTESVILLE & LONDON

University of Virginia Press
© 2013 by Donald McCaig
All rights reserved

Printed in the United States of America
on acid-free paper

First published 2013
ISBN 978-0-8139-3450-1
1 3 5 7 9 8 6 4 2

Library of Congress Cataloging-in-Publication Data
is available from the Library of Congress.

FOR
Rachael Ashley-Layton
&
June

If a fool would persist in his folly
he would become wise.
WILLIAM BLAKE

───────

Humans are a lonely species.
Dogs were our first friends.
VICKI HEARNE

Contents

MR. AND MRS. DOG

West Texas

Billy Bob's West Texas high school hired a new English teacher;
a Yankee who liked to talk about "epiphanies." She used the word
in every other sentence. Puzzled, Billy Bob went to the dictionary.

Next morning, when the teacher discovered another "epiphany,"
Billy Bob raised his hand. "Ma'am," he said, "There ain't no 'epiphanies' in West Texas. Hell, it's two hundred miles to the nearest
'coincidence.'"

I AM A VISIONARY. Not the "visionary" CEO grinning from the cover
of your seatback magazine, much less a Joseph Smith or Isaiah. I am a
run-of-the-mill visionary: plain vanilla. When I was younger, I didn't
discriminate between visions produced by decades of spiritual discipline
and visions got by swallowing a pill. I became a pharmacological tourist in
the iridescent world where William Blake communed with angels.

Visions are not created equal. Some altered the way I saw the world,
others how I feared it. Some of the best were funny. I recall one fine fall
afternoon in Detroit's inner city when I'd ground, boiled, encapsulated,
and ingested (at the time legal) mail-order peyote and was dissolving into
Brahms's *German Requiem* when fire erupted in the mortuary school
across the street. The cinematic confusion — fire trucks, flames, and bus-
tling undertaker trainees each in white shirt and somber black suit — was,
since I'm not William Blake, indescribable.

Visions are not created equal. A jiggling highway center line is banal.
A center line melding with the shoulder line is a headache. It was January and I was heading to West Texas for the Sheepdog Winter Olympics,
sixteen hundred miles from home, right now outside Texarkana. "In those
old cotton fields back home" — damned if I could get the tune out of my
head — "just about a mile from Texarkana." I needed a rest stop, but if
Texas had any, they were deep in the heart of . . . Quit it! Just quit!

I'd dozed at midnight shivering under my jacket at a Tennessee rest stop. I woke to a white world: my and the dogs' breath had frosted the inside of the windshield. I scraped icy slivers onto the dash.

Four-thirty a.m. That damned center line wouldn't stop flopping around and how to stay awake until daybreak? Where was that truck stop? Remember when truck stop coffee tasted like dog piss? Luke and June were zoned out in the wagon's wayback. They'd keep until the sun came up.

I've an old friend who's abused every substance known to the DEA and some they haven't heard about. His interest is both practical and theoretical; he's worked needle exchanges and taken intoxication seminars at Berkeley.

One spring he and his wife accompanied me to a sheepdog trial north of San Francisco. It was young June's first trial and we were DQed in less than thirty seconds.

That evening over dinner, when I tried to explain what it was like when it went *well* — the pure focus and swiftness of handling a sheepdog — my friend snickered. "Bullshit," he said. "You just like to get stoned."

He may have had a point. The dogs and I were traveling twenty-six hours in a twenty-year-old station wagon to get ready for a trial on the other side of the Atlantic. I had this vision, you see. Next October at Llandielo, Carmarthenshire, Wales, I would step onto that lush green British field with Luke or June and there'd be white sheep in the distance. It'd be cool; might be a breeze blowing. My dog and I would glance at one another. That glance was as particular and as far as my vision could carry me: to the intimate silence just before everything gets real.

Me and the dogs hit Dallas during the morning rush and the old wagon's temp gauge shot up but dropped after I killed the AC. The Texas speed limit shot up to seventy-five outside of Midland.

Midland, Texas, is ugly. Poor folks' homes are smaller and shabbier than in Appalachia. Dirt roads lead to oil wells protected by razor wire and wind turbines clutter the ridge tops, thousands of wind turbines. I wouldn't want to be a bird in Midland, Texas.

I STOPPED TO PHONE my hostess, Sarah Boudreau: did she want me to pick up groceries? Just outside of Sheffield, Texas, I'd pass Hayre Headquarters Ranch, turn left at the Las Norias sign, pass through the "bump gate," and I'd be there.

Bump gate?

South of Midland the topography didn't soften: rimrocks, chalky soil from which plants made a stand with mean-ass thorns and spikes. Natural desolation isn't as ugly as manmade.

Eighty-mile-per-hour limit on US 10. West Texas crude was fetching $160 a barrel and most traffic was drilling and oil service trucks. Road shoulders were mowed thirty feet back so drivers had a sporting chance to miss the deer who lacking better forage grazed on them.

Sheffield, Texas, had one gas station and one abandoned auto court. A couple hundred Sheffieldians did what for a living I couldn't guess. Sheffield did have a school. Maybe everybody worked at the school. Maybe producing and schooling children provided Sheffield's economic base. Stop it! I was very tired.

In midafternoon I got to Las Norias ("the wells"— gas, not water wells), where I learned a "bump gate" is a pipe gate you smack with your front bumper so it swings open and you zip through before the gate swings back to dent your car. At the farmhouse, I shut down and the car ticked and bubbled. The dogs were glad to get out of the car. Me too.

LAS NORIAS, one of three Hayre ranches, runs for miles along both sides of the road and five or six miles deep.

For decades, they raised sheep. One bad drought year, after the Texas grass was finished, the Hayres shipped forty thousand sheep to South Dakota for graze. "We had six semis," Bud Boudreau told me, "that went back for another load as soon as the sheep were off-loaded." When the government's wool incentive payment ended, Hayre's sheep were sold. Today the Hayres own I didn't ask how many cattle and fifteen thousand goats — and, oh yes, all those oil and gas wells. Bud helps with gathers and shearing but mostly he trains the ranch's stockdogs.

Las Norias's ranch house was built in the 1930s with two-foot-thick concrete walls and heavy steel shutters over each window. I wondered what kind of weather might demand such protection. When I described the ranch house to a Big Bend National Park ranger, he suggested, "Bandits?" I'm still not sure he was kidding.

FOR THIRTY YEARS Bud Boudreau made a good living as a racetrack farrier, but he quit when he could no longer stomach how the horses were treated. Bud got into sheepdogs about the same time I did, and moved to South Dakota where he reared, trained, and sold dogs. Later he lived on a big Argentine estancia, training dogs and teaching gauchos how to use them. Now, he and Sarah summer on their South Dakota spread — which becomes Hayre Ranch's summer headquarters — and winter at Las Norias.

Sarah and Bud's romance was like something out of a country song. On Bud's advice, classical musician Sarah sold her French horn to buy her first sheepdog. When Bud phoned to tell her he'd been wrong, the dog was useless, Sarah already owned it.

"Oh yeah," Bud told me. "Sarah used to get all these phone calls from the Dallas Symphony, all those places."

Although they lived far apart, they were an item until the day Bud drove in to a trial Sarah was judging and discovered that Sarah'd married someone else who wasn't even a sheepdogger!

Thinking fast, Bud picked wildflowers and put them in a pop bottle in the judge's portopot.

Sarah said, "That's the best you can do? Flowers in an outhouse?"

But somehow Bud's hapless gesture did the trick. Bud bought the new husband an airline ticket home and married Sarah himself.

THE KAYCEE sheepdog trial is *the* big whoop-up in the tiny Wyoming town whose most famous citizens were Butch Cassidy and the Sundance Kid. There's a lamb cook-off, sheepshearing, herders' wagons, a street dance, and bagpiping. The New Zealand shearers working in Kaycee that summer proposed a novel contest. Teams would form and climb onto a flatbed truck. Best time wins. GO! The first competitor shears a sheep. As soon as the ewe is denuded, his teammate eats a large bowl of unmoistened bran flakes. When his bowl is empty, the third man chokes down a dry twelve-inch pancake and, racing for the finish, the last one chugalugs a quart of beer. The fourth contestant must be a girl.

Sheepshearers have an odd sense of humor.

The sheepdogger team devised a bold strategy: their "girl" would be Stormy Winters, a fifty-year-old, bowlegged, Canadian bronc buster. Miss Stormy would make up so much time in the chugalugging, the sheepdoggers had a lock. In Kaycee's general store they bought a blond wig and a big enough dress, although they couldn't zip up the back.

When Miss Stormy climbed onto the flatbed some bigmouth kid shrieked, "It's Shrek! It's Shrek!"

Their subterfuge undetected and the stopwatch set, the sheepdog team made their play. Sheep sheared, bran flakes choked down, and Bud grabbed a twelve-inch dry pancake.

Alas, nobody had recalled Bud's swallowing history. Last spring he'd got a peanut caught in his throat, choked, and nearly blacked out. In Kaycee, although Bud chewed and chewed his throat muscles wouldn't contract.

With victory so close she could taste it, Miss Stormy smacked Bud on the back, hollering, "Swallow the fucking thing! Swallow the fucking thing!"

Despite Miss Stormy's Olympic-speed chugalug, the sheepdogger team finished fourth.

Sarah Boudreau informed her husband, "Honey, you were the weak link."

THE SHEEPDOG TRIAL is as time-honored and rough as the shepherd who after too many pints slaps his wages on the bar and proclaims, "My dog is a damn sight more useful than yours."

That's it. The sheepdog trial is a contest of farm and ranch dogs doing the same work they do every day at home. It's a simple test: dog runs out, gathers sheep, and fetches them to his shepherd. Dog drives the sheep through obstacles. Then dog and man sort the sheep and pen them. Any halfway decent sheepdog can do it but some are better than others.

Sheepdog trials were formalized in Britain and its sheepier colonies in the nineteenth century. Far as I know, the first US sheepdog trial was at the 1893 Columbian Exposition.

These days there are thousands of trials in the UK, Australia, Europe, Brazil, North America, South Africa, Scandinavia, the Falklands, and New Zealand. They're held pretty much anywhere with great numbers of sheep tended by just a few shepherds. The most important trials are our National Finals, the Canadian Championship, the European Championship, the North and South Island Championships (New Zealand), and the British International where teams compete from England, Scotland, Ireland, and Wales.

The World Trials is the newest top trial and — despite Britain's "International"— the only truly international sheepdog trial. Next fall, the best sheepdoggers from twenty-two nations would gather in Llandielo, South Wales, for one hell of a sheepdog trial. I yearned to be among them.

Some visionaries are just plain stupid (google: neoconservative). Stupid visionaries may outnumber percipient ones and though some visions are inspired, more are hallucinations.

My plan was simplicity itself. First, qualify for the United States Team; second, get Mr. and Mrs. Dog to the UK. After we got to South Wales there'd be the little matter of two hundred of the best sheepdogs and handlers in the world to worry about, but puh-leeze! one thing at a time!

The dogs and I had work to do, which was why I was lying half-asleep deep in West Texas at four in the morning listening to Bud playing meditative guitar in the other room. I recognized Segovia-influenced Bach and — wasn't that "America the Beautiful"?

LUCERO DE LA MAÑANA was gleaming on the horizon when Bud and I went out to introduce Luke, June, and Donald to goats. We were in a flat pasture, maybe eighty acres, where Bud informed me, "The wind is coming from the north and the goats'll be facing into it. There! See them in that fence corner?"

Nope.

After Bud sent his dog into the dimness and goats didn't appear, he told me some goat had probably got her horns stuck in the fence, and Bud disappeared too.

I couldn't see squat. I gave Bud a couple minutes to extricate the goat before sending June. No point uttering commands when I didn't know what was going on: it was up to June. Directly she brought a hundred goats.

When he appeared, Bud said there were two goats stuck in the fence. "June waited them out. She was patient and sensible."

Goats are flightier than sheep and much too clever for their rank in the food chain. Goats scream if a dog nips them. Some dogs learn to enjoy that scream.

AFTER THE DOGS and I made our acquaintance with goats, Bud asked, "Do you want to bring the sheep off the rimrock?"

Behind the ranch house, equipment sheds, and bunkhouses, a western-movie mesa maybe five hundred feet high loomed over Las Norias. "See the sheep?" Bud pointed at, er . . . nothing.

In this unfamiliar terrain, I had a tourist's eyes. Nope. Don't see no sheep.

Impatiently: "There they are, right on top. You want to send your dog?"

I've failed too many times to fear failure. I walked Luke toward the base of the steep scree slope above which were sheep somewhere. Luke looked at it and looked back at me: "You sure 'bout this?"

I insisted and Luke started his climb; a second insist and he clambered over the top and vanished. Bud thought he could see the top of Luke's head. "It's the only round thing up there," he noted.

After a couple minutes sheep appeared on the rim but I couldn't see Luke so I gave a "walk up" whistle to let him know I hadn't forgotten him. Another whistle. I could more or less guess what Luke was doing by how the sheep moved.

The mesa was broken by near perpendicular cliffs. "Don't worry," Bud reassured me, "the sheep can find their way down."

And my dog?

Flocklets broke off and back up the slope. I gave Luke his "look back" whistle and he scrambled after the outlaws.

Four years ago Luke was the dog who wouldn't go out for sheep he couldn't see. That day, he made invisible sheep visible and fetched them to our feet. Luke's tongue was hanging out. He was delighted with himself. My dogs love this work as much as I do.

THE FIRST TRIAL of the Texas Sheepdog Winter Olympics was in a hundred-acre field previously irrigated for alfalfa and surrounded by ten-foot fences to keep the deer from gobbling same. Absent irrigation, the field became an enormous chalk tennis court invaded by ferocious, spiky West Texas vegetation. Red electrical cords crisscrossed the ground. Electrical cords? Huh? Some sort of West Texas thing?

The truck stop fronting the field was a double-wide improved by three plastic tables where you could eat your microwaved burger and walls covered with posters for indie rock bands. The bands had self-conscious, too clever names, and a revolving rack of forlorn CDs separated the beer cooler from the motor oils. Outside this outpost of civilization some semis snoozed and we sheepdoggers trialed our dogs.

Hub Holmes is a lifelong Texas rancher. When somebody asked Hub why so many West Texans wear black Stetsons, Hub replied, "Monkey see, monkey do."

When Hub and his dog Dave came off the field at a New England trial, a woman objected. "Hub, you've been calling your dog 'Day-ave.' 'Dave' is just one syllable."

"Oh shay-it," Hub replied.

In 1991, the National Finals were held in Sheridan, Wyoming, and since my *Eminent Dogs, Dangerous Men* had just been published, I convinced the publisher to fly me and my gyp Gael to Billings, Montana, for power interviews with the *Billings Gazette* and several rural radio stations before driving to Sheridan for the trial.

(So they can talk dogs when ladies are present southern bird dog men call their females *gyps.* Since modern, vulgar misuses of *bitch* demean all femininity, *gyp* is more courteous.)

Sheridan was my first National Finals and I didn't know if I belonged there. Turned out: I didn't. The course was on a polo field flat as a billiard table, and that was only one reason Gael and I ran so poorly. After we came off I asked Hub, "What did I do wrong?"

"You got off the plane."

Hub's wife, Allison, is Canadian born. After they married, Hub fetched his bride to the Holmes ranch through eight bump gates, forty miles from the paved road. Hub's father, Harry, stepped out to greet the newlyweds. He looked Allison up and down. "Canadian, huh? I'll bet you're one of those damn tree huggers."

Allison exploded, "If I ever see a tree in this godforsaken country, you bet your ass I'd hug it." Which marked the beginning of a beautiful friendship.

Hub is president of the United States Border Collie Handlers' Association (aka USBCHA or HA) and past president of the registry, the American Border Collie Association (ABCA). Hub is fair-minded, unexcitable, and gets things done.

Like George W. Bush, Francis Raley has a ranch outside Crawford, Texas, and if you don't mention Francis's neighbor you won't get an earful. She's secretary-for-life of the Texas Sheepdog Association and the HA but won't take a penny for her work. "You couldn't pay me enough to make it worthwhile." At that Sheridan Finals, I was whining to Francis about how much sheepdog trialing costs. "Without the dogs I could afford a new Subaru."

Francis calculated. "A Mercedes," she corrected me.

Emil Luedeke breeds and trains some of the best sheepdogs in Texas (some say North America). Emil invariably wears faded coveralls and battered work boots and doesn't trim his bushy white beard. To their subsequent regret, some dog buyers have underestimated Emil.

Last season, Emil and Bud had been ragging on each other, trial after trial, just driving each other nuts. At the Pecos River Trial, the goats were unwilling to pen and nobody succeeded until Emil.

After Emil penned, he started toward Bud, and Bud just knew Emil was going to crow and run shit so Bud did what a man's got to do. He dropped trou and mooned Emil.

The next morning Bud came late to the handlers' meeting. (As handlers warm their hands on their coffee cups the course director describes the course.) That particular morning, forty Texas hats clustered around Hub and Francis when Bud arrived. All eyes were on Bud.

Hub and Francis seemed puzzled by a letter Hub was holding. He asked, "I haven't got my reading glasses. Bud, will you read this aloud?"

"You bet."

To whom it may concern.

Yesterday, on our way to the Pecos Baptist Convention we pulled off US 10 for gasoline and a snack. The proprietor of the Pecos River Truckstop mentioned an event my daughters, aged six and nine, might enjoy. There were sheepdogs competing in the field behind and since my daughters love animals, I said they could go watch for a while.

Not ten minutes later, the girls returned sobbing bitterly. Instead of the innocent exhibition I had imagined, these maidens saw a naked man flaunting his private parts. Although the eldest child may recover, the younger has been severely traumatized. Our attorney says . . .

"Jeez," Bud says. "The tears were running down my face. Here I'd traumatized two young girls! Why was everybody laughing? Francis and Hub had stayed up half the night concocting the darn thing . . ."

THE BLACKTOP speed limit was seventy-five and when you're passing at eighty plus, that oncoming dot on the horizon becomes a hulking seismograph truck faster than you can spit. Most West Texas trucks have serious steel bullbars beat to shit. My old wagon didn't have a bullbar and though I've hit deer I've never hit one at eighty miles per hour. No, I didn't slow down.

The dogs and I drove to Big Bend National Park which is, I was informed, "the least visited" National Park, which wasn't hard to understand. Big Bend is stunningly beautiful desolation on the banks of the unswimmable, undrinkable Rio Grande. Prickly pear, yucca, creosote bush, and big and little cacti claw for life and the guidebook urges hikers to not drink too much at the rare springs as desert creatures need the water too. It further advised that I might meet illegals who might ask me for water. Instead I should report them to the authorities. You betcha.

This country scared me. On the two-lane highway snaking toward park headquarters I saw exactly one other car. Gravel byways offered passage to this or that attraction, natural formation, or view, but I was not tempted. With two dogs and one gallon of drinking water in my aged station wagon, I clung to civilized pavement.

When I got to headquarters and asked why Big Bend is a desert, a ranger helpfully explained, "Because we don't get much rain."

When he was US secretary of war, Jefferson Davis tested a camel corps here. Camels could eat the ubiquitous and to most species unpalatable creosote bush. Camels didn't need much water. His plan worked better than the Confederacy.

I had a sudden vision: Donald the Rich Entrepreneur! Camels! I'd start small with tame camels. Let them gobble creosote bush and hoard water on cheap West Texas land. I'd become "the Camel Man" introducing succulent camel hump steaks to Whole Foods and Trader Joe's!

Alas, visions are not created equal.

AT THE SHEFFIELD TRIAL, goats were set out five hundred yards from the handler's post. I couldn't see the goats through the thick brush, but they'd be somewhere near the setout man and I could see his horse.

Remember those red electric cords? They connected seismograph sensors and as June and I stepped onto the course, a seismograph truck raised its mighty thumper. KER-WHUMP. Strobe lights flashed as it sent shock waves to its sensors. KER-WHUMP.

June couldn't see any sheep or goats but by God she sure could see that thumper truck. She locked on like a thumper-seeking missile. I set June up to outrun on the other side from the truck. I set her up to run on the other side but had this sinking feeling . . .

June wanted, nay NEEDED to fetch that big thumping, flickering weirdness and nothing I said — neither my shouts nor redirects — swayed June from her goal. When a sheepdog starts on one side but crosses to the other, it's a killer fault — you lose so many points there's no reason to keep trying.

June arrived at the truck and looked around at me. What the hey?

Smarty-pants and I retired and as we walked off, Bud called, "Sorry about that truck."

"What would you rather have: a dog that can find goats or a dog that can find oil?"

Luke, June, and I had epiphanies in West Texas. The umpteenth time they offered a paw so I could extract sand burrs, the dogs learned they couldn't put their feet down just any old place. Not in West Texas they couldn't.

My mother used to tell me I should "learn from my mistakes." At the Pecos River Trial, the day after June tried to gather the seismograph truck, I set her up again on the left side assuming she'd learned, "No goats out there yesterday. Ergo: no goats today."

Nope. June promptly crossed a second time and ran to where the seismograph truck had been. Same "what the hey?" Same retired.

Sorry, Ma. Like us, dogs learn from their successes. We and they fall in love with our mistakes.

The Education of
a Dog Man

T HE DOGCATCHER was the most hated man in my hometown. In the 1940s and '50s Butte, Montana, was a one-industry mining town. If you didn't want to go down the holes, jobs were scarce and town jobs were real plums. But Butte's dogcatcher was appointed in a closed meeting of the city council and his name wasn't revealed. Despite these precautions, pretty soon everybody knew which son-of-a-bitch had the dirty job and most dogcatchers only lasted a month or two. It wasn't the slashed tires on the (unmarked) official van that forced them out. It was the slashed tires on their personal cars.

Most Butte families had a dog or two and most dogs ran free. A pack accompanied our mailman on his rounds. Dogs joined up when the mailman came into their neighborhood and fell away when he passed into the next. Two regulars, a big red dog and a small yellow gyp, walked his entire round.

Our family dogs were strays my mother fed for a day or two or a week before they wandered off. Rover and Susie and Spot were the strays I remember. Our back gate was chalked with hobo hieroglyphs which promised that Ma was a soft touch. Apparently stray dogs could read hobo marks too.

Sometime after the war my parents bought a "better" dog, a purebred registered with the American Kennel Club. Rascal, a forty-pound Cocker Spaniel, became my buddy. I was a solitary kid, and nights I wasn't curled around a book I would amble through the sleeping city, through mine yards, along railroad tracks, through back alleys, lost in my visions of glory. Rascal always came too. On bitter January days, ice would ball up between his toes and I'd sling my dog around my neck and carry him home.

I don't remember training him. I don't think my parents or I believed a dog needed training. Rascal came when called, sat, and shook hands, didn't mess in the house, fight other dogs, bark stupidly, or bite people.

When I was sixteen and Rascal was six, I bought a '48 Dodge sedan with money I'd earned delivering for the corner drugstore. I had a car, a dog, and a hundred bucks, and June first, the day after school got out, Rascal and I left for Glacier Park three hundred miles north.

My parents thought I'd soon run out of money and come home. They didn't figure on the kind strangers who fed the scrawny kid and his dog all summer. I wrote two postcards. Hell, I knew we were doing Great!

Rascal and I hiked the high trails and slept in the car. Rascal barked at a bear raiding my larder and I threw a pot at it. Come Labor Day, I had enough money left to get home provided I saved gas coasting eighteen miles down the Going to the Sun Highway. When I reached Butte my brakes were burned up and my father was too. He had the state police looking for me.

I was indignant. School didn't start until TOMORROW!

Even as a kid I was a pain in the ass.

I don't think Butte had a dog trainer. It didn't need one. You couldn't get up much speed on the hilly streets, drivers anticipated dogs and kids dashing out, and my mother, like most mothers, was home all day. Rascal was as well trained as any dog in Butte. Somehow, after Rascal died I lost touch with dogs.

I was thirty years old when my wife, Anne, and I moved to a run-down sheep farm in a beautiful, sparsely populated Appalachian county. Anne's parents had been over-fastidious and as a child she'd never had a dog. I answered a "Free to Good Home" ad for the Labrador/Chesapeake Bay Retriever we named Lucille. Lucille was a calm, kind, philosophical dog. I was correcting her one day when my friend Dan Way gave me my first dog training lesson. "You can't be saying 'No' all the time. Sometimes you have to say 'Yes.'"

Rusty — Anne's cousin's Brittany Spaniel — lived with us while his young owner sorted himself out. One day Checkers, our Holstein steer, charged Rusty — half in play, half for real — the way young cattle will. At the last possible instant, Rusty shot him a *meaningful* glance and Checkers veered off: "No offense, man. I didn't mean to step in your shit."

Lucille died young of cancer; Rusty went deaf and didn't hear the car that killed him.

By then I was making a scant living writing and we owned a hundred and fifty ewes that came to the barn at feeding time or when we rattled corn in a bucket. *If* they felt like it. When we needed to worm our three-hundred-forty-pound rams we crept up on the sleeping beasts and pounced before they could get to their feet.

I told Anne, "I think we need a working dog."

"Sure," Anne agreed. "But where can we find a dog that can type?"

I hadn't bought Anne a birthday present and a friend was going to pick up a Border Collie pup at the state fair. "Buy me one too," I said. Ignorance is sometimes rewarded and that black-and-white puppy (Anne said Pip looked like "a rat in a tuxedo") changed how we farmed, inspired *Nop's Trials,* my first best-seller, and changed our life.

We writers are jackdaws, collecting this pretty bauble and that charming gewgaw to decorate our visions. I fall in love easily. I fall out of love easily too and I assumed sheepdogs would join the junk heap of my previous enthusiasms. I am astonished that thirty years later I still train, work, and trial sheepdogs.

I didn't win my first open trial until I'd been trialing ten years, but eventually I became a fair handler and my life (literally) went to the dogs. I have no dog-allergic friends. I stay with friends or family going to or from sheepdog trials and my literary agent and I confer outdoors in Central Park with Mr. and Mrs. Dog tucked under the bench beside us.

Last September I had a colonoscopy and was half-conscious and bare-arsed on the table, when a nurse fumbled with the lanyard around my neck. "What's this?" she asked.

I never know when I might need my dog whistle.

Every dog culture — bird dogs, obedience dogs, show dogs, sled dogs, search and rescue — every dog culture is insular. We're so busy with our own dogs we haven't time for (or much interest in) different cultures. Few top sheepdog handlers have ever seen a dog show, and most AKC show

Border Collie judges have never seen sheepdogs do the work they were bred to do.

I didn't know anything about the "dog fancy" until the American Kennel Club began stalking the Border Collie. Sheepdoggers' attempt to forestall AKC "recognition" of our Border Collies dragged me from my comfort zone into different dog cultures — with all the enthusiasm of a hard-shell Baptist at Muslim prayers. I even attended the Westminster Kennel Club's dog show, which was depressing. Some perfectly decent dog lovers were in thrall to an authoritarian registry awarding blue ribbons to far too many desperately unsound dogs. Breeding for dog shows is so obviously bad for dogs and those who own and love them, I cannot understand how otherwise rational human beings can defend the practice.

The upside of the fight (we lost) was the new friends I made in non-sheepdog cultures and the brilliant pet dog trainers I got to know. They understood things about dogs I did not.

I'm a sheepdog trainer, not a pet dog trainer. This may seem too punctilious: dogs are dogs, right?

Learning to work a sheepdog takes a decade or so — unless you've trained horses. The ex–horse trainer's learning curve is almost always shorter. Since Vicki Hearne trained dogs and horses for movie work, I asked her why.

Vicki laughed. "That's easy. You can't be stupid with a horse; horses can kill you. You can be very stupid with a dog."

Dogs let us believe whatever we want to believe. They are brilliant enablers. Want to see your dog as a person in a dog suit? Woof woof!

A fur baby? Arf!

Offering unconditional luv? Bow-wow!

Human fantasies about them are often dogs' only currency. When rock drummer Keith Moon destroyed a hotel room, he could buy his way out. If your dog wrecks a hotel room, his next stop may be the animal shelter. Most dogs relinquished to animal shelters are killed for problem behaviors much, much milder than Mr. Moon's.

Canis familiarus threw in his lot with *Homo sapiens sapiens* some hundred thousand years ago when glaciers slid into France and pushed the cold-adapted Neanderthals as far south as modern Israel. In this same period the Sahara, which had blocked hominid migrations out of Africa, got an unusual amount of rainfall, and a small group of our ancestors — perhaps only one band of two or three families — got through the Sahara into the fertile Levant.

Although *Homo sapiens sapiens* had known African canids — jackals and wild dogs — he hadn't met wolves and couldn't have greeted them enthusiastically. That small wolf — the modern dog's ancestor — is extinct, but short-coated, prick-eared, red-brown village dogs found on every continent probably resemble him.

The dog that adopted man weighed about forty pounds and had a nose that functioned like radar; when the wind was right, the dog could detect food or danger almost a mile away. His hearing was much more acute than man's and in dim light he saw better. He could sprint twice as fast — thirty-five miles an hour. He could hunt for two or three days without food or water. He had slashing teeth and strong bone-crunching jaws and his powers were multiplied in a pack of dogs, or a pack of men and dogs.

Man and Dog formed a formidable partnership. Man's cunning combined with Dog's senses and physical abilities to create a wonderful evolutionary symbiosis. Since Dog could hear the faintest whisper of danger, for the first time, men could rest. Dog brought Man a better diet. Dog fought other humans and Neanderthals and protected the humans' children. The most precious gift Dog gave Man was time: time to think, to consider; time to make art; time to pray.

The dog, like us, is a cooperative hunter; like us it's a pack animal. Some dog trainers insist your pet has its own agenda and in small ways that's true, but if your pet's ancestor had attacked your ancestor's child, that dog wouldn't have survived to breed.

There are Lord knows how many dog breeds but there are no breed differences so profound as those distinguishing dog from wolf. As Michael Pollan notes in *The Botany of Desire,* "There are fifty million dogs in America today, only ten thousand wolves. So what does the dog know about getting along in this world that its wild ancestor doesn't? The big thing the dog knows about — the subject it has mastered in the . . . years it has been evolving at our side — is us: our needs and desires, our emotions and values, all of which it has folded into its genes as part of a sophisticated strategy for survival."

Our ancestors were lanky and relatively frail, physically weaker than the Neanderthals. *Homo sapiens* had smaller teeth, a poorer sense of smell, and perhaps weaker eyesight. Both hominid species probably possessed speech, though some skeletal evidence suggests that Neanderthal speech may have been less complex. Both had fire and used identical techniques to manufacture stone tools and butchering implements. Probably *Homo sapiens* was more nomadic than the Neanderthals. The Neanderthals had slightly bigger brains.

Seventy-four thousand years ago when Sumatra's Mount Toba erupted, volcanic ash blocked sunlight and lowered summer temperatures twelve degrees. Think nuclear winter. *Homo sapiens* crashed from 100,000 to 10,000 individuals. Friends, we too have been an endangered species. Yet in an age that would know many periods of brutal cold, the less adapted *Homo sapiens* survived while the last Neanderthal died fifteen thousand years before his rival invented agriculture.

Cal Tech neurobiologist John Allman speculates that we thin-skinned humans replaced cold-tolerant Neanderthals during the last ice age because we had dogs and Neanderthals did not.

Overcoming the
Home Court Advantage

To MOST PEOPLE, "sheep" is synonymous with "stupid." Murrow's "a nation of sheep" is no compliment. Yet, to my knowledge, no sheep in North America believed Saddam Hussein had weapons of mass destruction. None invested with Bernie Madoff.

These tests aside, sheep are extremely good at being sheep. They bed down on high ground and post sentries for predator alerts. Mamas teach their lambs to shun poisonous plants, and sheep are much better than we at evaluating dogs. The same sheep that will quietly go where directed by an experienced sheepdog will break fences in a panic if an unruly pet is turned loose on them.

Sheep were originally adapted to unique regional circumstances and they retain behavioral genetics from those origins. Since Scottish Black-faces graze very poor browse they keep a distance one from another. They are easily shed, but hard to gather and keep together. Our Rambouilet-cross sheep were so "flocky" that if we put a sick ewe into the barn for treatment, we'd always include a second sheep as a companion. Cheviots are fast, "light" (easy to move) sheep. Suffolks are "heavy" (harder to move). Hair sheep tolerate stress more easily than wool sheep. In New England, sheepdogs usually work well-dogged, one-hundred-twenty-pound hair sheep: Katahdins, St. Croix, or Barbados Blackbellies. In the West, they'll work undogged one-hundred-sixty-pound Rambouillets and Rambouillet crosses. Western sheep may have never seen a man who wasn't on horseback and the last dog they saw was the coyote eating their mama.

A New England trial dog may not have the authority to control wild western sheep and a western sheepdog may not have the precision needed to win the Skowhegan State Fair trial in Maine.

A few years ago, several top British sheepdog handlers were invited to bring their dogs to Utah for the Soldier Hollow trial. Since the Meeker, Colorado, trial was the following weekend, they signed up for it too. At Soldier Hollow, spooky range sheep are turned loose on a big chunk of prairie. These experienced Brits with their brilliant dogs were skunked, so badly beaten they cancelled Meeker and went home with their collective tails between their legs.

For you, me, and my sheepdogs, the world differs more vitally than we usually credit. My Highland County neighbors think Manhattan is Sodom or (in a more charitable mood) Gomorrah. Manhattanites assume my neighbors know nothing and impregnate their sisters. Our commonplace chauvinisms demonstrate how particular geographies define our sensibilities. Some downtown New Yorkers rarely cross Fourteenth Street into hoity-toity uptown. Highland County families came here in the 1790s when Monterey, the county seat, was settled by Germans and Williamsville, forty minutes south, by Scotch-Irish. A Monterey preacher told me, "Growing up in the '60s I was told: 'It's okay to fool around with a Scotch-Irish girl, but you'll marry a German.'" Rules and cues vary more than we self-espoused democrats pretend. There is no place on earth where it's good to be a stranger.

I'd never been to South Wales. I didn't know whether the soil was sweet or sour nor which forbs thrived and which wouldn't grow. Neither my dogs nor I knew how light and shadow interacted on a summer evening there nor how dewy grass smelled. Llandielo, in far-off South Wales, would have its unique secrets when my dog and I stepped onto an unfamiliar trial field to work Welsh Mountain Sheep, a breed we'd never worked, against the best sheepdogs and handlers in the world.

To have a hope, Luke, June, and I had to become master adapters. We had to take in novel information swiftly and assimilate it instantly into our work patterns. We had to expect the unfamiliar and produce strategies for reducing the new to the matter-of-fact.

Adaptive skills couldn't be trained. We'd learn to adapt by frequently adapting. For the next eighteen months the dogs and I would work unfamiliar sheep on unfamiliar terrain against the best dogs in North America.

They'd run on California desert and in the shadow of New Hampshire's White Mountains. They'd outwit gators in Florida canals and splash in the St. Lawrence and the Neversink. They'd work Rambouillet, Katahdin, Tunis, Barbados Blackbelly, Cheviot, Dorset, Suffolk, Polypay, and St. Croix sheep. This broad range of experience just might create dog (and human) strategies for dealing with the unfamiliar, the mentally challenging, and the emotionally fraught.

Unpredictablity was predictable. While I was walking dogs at the crack of dawn, outside Bowman, North Dakota (site of the the Slash J trial), Luke and June disappeared into the prairie: tall grass emptiness miles and miles north to the Canadian border. I whistled for my dogs. I called. I was breathing very fast. When Luke and June finally reappeared, they fetched a cow elk with them.

If we couldn't work Welsh Mountain Sheep or know what Welsh gorse felt like under our feet, we *could* become swifter learners. By supercharging the subconscious understandings upon which workaday understanding rests we'd be prepared to absorb the new.

That was the theory anyway.

Sheepdog trialing is a mental game. The dogs must understand and react appropriately to sheep and handler cues. The handler must unite cues from sheep breed, individual dog and sheep temperaments, lay of the land, weather, and time of day.

Some handlers are very, very good at this. The Bluegrass is a big, tough, important American trial. Alasdair MacRae (who has won the British International and our National Finals) had drawn an early slot. Sheep set out early in the morning are likely to be relatively easier to handle — those ewes who evade the pen workers to lurk in the back of the pen until day's end are ovine bad actors. Morning is cool and less stressful for sheep and dogs and the sheep's bellies are full.

That particular June morning a faint haze hung over the letout pens, five hundred fifty yards out from the handler's post. When someone congratulated Alasdair on his early morning draw he demurred. "In this haze I cannot make out the sheep's ears."

Whoa. While a sheep's ear set does indicate her intentions, these ears were four or five inches long and five hundred yards away. At that distance, I can see sheep but can't determine whether there are three, four, or five of them. Wee little ear set? Not on the best day of my life.

That was the sort of talent we had to beat to earn a slot on the United States Team, and if the Mister, the Missus, and I hurdled that hurdle, the best dog/handler teams in the world were waiting for us in Wales.

I'd been coached by terrific sheepdog coaches. The lenses through which I saw sheepdogs had been ground and polished by world-class sheepdoggers. But too often at trials I was misreading my dog.

Misreading? Hmm. The best pet dog trainers have trained or helped train thirty thousand dogs. These trainers talk dog, they dance dog, they sing dog. They've dedicated their lives to dogs and to teaching the dogs' fractious, often difficult owners. When it comes to dogs, they have seen everything.

They may have never worked sheepdogs but, by God, they do know how to read *your* dog

Could I learn from them? Might their insights help me see my own dogs better?

A couple years ago, noticing that most top handlers wore shooting glasses, a novice asked Scott Glenn what colored lenses she should buy.

"Rose-colored," Scott deadpanned.

I needed to change my lenses, to learn how to see my dogs afresh. Maybe I could borrow the pet dog trainers' lenses.

To see my dogs better, I needed to learn to see your dog. Funny how things work out sometimes.

Mr. and Mrs. Dog

I T WAS ONE OF those fine, clear fall days when grimy old Manhattan is beautiful. Water taxis buzzed past the Hudson River Park, lovers of every persuasion made private spaces for billing and cooing. Children dashed, joggers puffed, and tai chi practitioners emulated herons. The dogs and I had found some shade. The pot dealer did a double take when he spotted Luke and June snoozing at my feet. "Them two, they brother and sister?"

"Dog and wife," I replied.

He nodded. Uh-huh.

I bought June when she was thirteen months old. I'd been seeking a started sheepdog when Florence Wilson told me her husband, Tommy, had a gyp he might be willing to sell. When Tommy worked June I saw: fast (maybe too fast — quick moves spook sheep), biddable (June took Tommy's commands without demur), and she was effortlessly athletic. June was "bareskinned" (smooth-coated), which makes for less burr-picking in the fall.

After I paid for my new dog, Florence informed me, "She has a wee bit too much eye." "Eye" is sheepdog-ese for the sheepdog's glare — the same blank, threatening stare street thugs intimidate you with. The sheepdog's eye intimidates and moves sheep. A "wee bit too much" means the dog might freeze or clap (lie down) and not get up again.

That wasn't June's worst fault. All her littermates were sold to trial handlers and every one had two flaws. The sheepdog's outrun to the sheep MUST NOT disturb the sheep, and, consequently, the dog must run wide — widest where it passes the sheep — before it turns in to slip up quietly behind them. June and her littermates preferred to charge straight at the sheep and circle behind at the last possible instant. Sheep hate a "fishhook" outrun and become unruly, but these young dogs did it because the sheep *did move*. So what if they were in a panic? At least they weren't stand-ing still with lowered heads, stamping the earth and threatening the dog.

And all June's litter were slow developers. June didn't really come into her own until she was four. I'm sentimental and Anne is terminally so; once a dog enters our house that dog stays. Sentimentality has forced me to become a patient, persistent trainer. Other handlers lost patience and of six littermates, only June and one other are still trialing.

June's virtues? She's clever, learns quickly from experience, and has be-come wise. At one South Carolina trial, the host's wife, a schoolteacher, invited me to speak to her class and I brought June along.

Turned out, it was a kindergarten and we walked into a roomful of short people. I was pleased when a teacher told them, "If any of you don't want the dog to come near, sit at this table and she won't bother you." A few did.

Most lined up as June flopped on her back and let each short person pat her belly. "Now Johnny, wash your hands. Mary, go wash your hands."

She lay there while thirty-five kids — including some from the don't-wanna table — patted her. She did not do so because she likes to lie submis-sively on her back while strangers fondle her. I don't think I've ever patted June's belly. June lay there because she intuited her duty and did it.

June's worked tough sheep in rain, snow, ice storms, and brain-sapping heat. After work on hot days, she flops down in the river, lapping water as she paddles about. She sleeps in our plumpest chair and rises, stretching languorously, long after our other dogs have hurried outside to pee. She's a foxy lady in a slinky black and white peignoir. Uncommonly charming, June invites caresses.

Because of her fetching ways, June became my literary dog and has ac-companied me to bookstores, libraries, and universities. In motel hallways, she assumes any open door is her room and marches right in, which amused a sales conference in Green Bay, Wisconsin, but annoyed a Baptist prayer breakfast in Charlotte, North Carolina.

June's a dominant gyp, an iron paw in a velvet glove. I enjoy watching forty-five-pound June try to intimidate Ruth, our one-hundred-twenty-pound sheep-guarding dog. All ruffed up, June struts around her enor-mous rival while Ruth — cool as a moose — gives June *that* look: "Honey, who you tryin' to bullshit?"

June can read sheep, other dogs, and human beings. One afternoon, I was sitting outside a New Jersey motel drinking beer with dog show people. Their dogs were confined in portable wire kennels, but June was loose. Man pulled up and slipped into a room. Woman arrived separately and beelined for the room. June, who never barks at anyone, raised Holy Hell. Poor woman had intended Afternoon Delight with Inappropriate Other. She turned beet red, dashed to her car, and sped away. June sensed hanky-panky and let the world know about it.

Her cleverness has a downside. Since June doesn't get excited before her turn, I let her wait with me under the handlers' tent. Unfortunately, while I was gossiping, clever June was examining the field and making plans.

At big trials the sheep are often spotted where the dog can't see them and the handler cues the dog where they are with body language as the two walk to the post. Alas for our prospects, June had already decided where the sheep were and she ignored all my cues. She knew better! June has out-run to a white rock outcropping, several small white barns, and, once, kids next door playing volleyball. Her funniest mistake was that seismograph truck.

WHEREAS JUNE IS A secular rationalist, her spouse is a Calvinist. Luke isn't clever at all. He was not quite two years old the first time I was offered him. His owner sought a sentimental buyer who wouldn't sell Luke down the road. I didn't need another sheepdog but, okay, I'd take a look. When his owner tried to send Luke on an outrun, Luke wouldn't leave the man's feet, and I was glad to turn Luke down.

Two months later, June and I left a Connecticut nursery trial with a disappointing score, but a friend phoned later to say June had won it. Next morning, instead of driving home to Virginia, I returned to the trial and sure enough June had won.

The judge for the open class had cancelled unexpectedly so the trial host asked me to fill in.

The dog that impressed me most that day was young Luke. He'd trans-formed into a powerful, no-nonsense dog. The deal was done then and there. I opened his dog crate, which was bouncing up and down from Luke bouncing up and down inside it. My new dog jumped into the wagon and at the motel I discarded Luke's leash and discarded it has stayed.

LUKE WAS FOUR YEARS OLD before he trusted me enough to run out for sheep he couldn't see. When Luke was just eighteen months old, his trainer had entered him at Bloomfield, which boasts a six-hundred-yard outrun — much too big for a youngster. Worse, when Luke didn't find his sheep, the trainer ran at him, hollering and carrying on. Wrong message: Luke learned he might be sent where sheep couldn't be found and after he failed, his master would be angry at him.

It took time and patience to reset that particular doggy equation.

LUKE IS THE BEST SHEDDER I've ever owned ("shedding": sorting a ewe or ewes from a group) and has made some behind-my-back sheds that brought gasps from spectators. Luke is powerful. Horned rams eight times his size can't back him down. He's also pushy, adores me too much, and — Luke's a Blockhead.

Better handlers have offered to buy Luke from me and sometimes I've wished I'd sold him. He's tricky to handle. After his outrun (*running, running, running, free dog doing as he wishes, hahaha*) and he's four or five hundred yards out, Luke's hard to stop.

Whistles are gentler and more precise than voice commands — at distance, a shout is a shout is a SHOUT. But voice commands are more authoritative. If I SHOUT Luke off his feet, he thinks, "Ohmigod, the Boss is mad at me!" (Not good. Insecure Luke is less effective than Pushy Luke.) Luke is seven years old and for five of those years I've been trying to get him to stop when he gets behind his sheep. Ain't happened, probably ain't gonna happen. Compromise strategy: two hard "down" whistles and quieter "pause" whistles as he fetches the sheep, which segue into quiet voice commands — "Luke!" or "Take time!"— when he is near. If I can get Luke through the fetch without unnerving him, working together we can "lay one down" (do uncommonly elegant work). If I push the least bit too hard, Luke panics: he's failed to please.

MR. AND MRS. DOG

Luke has had Lyme disease, botulism (twice), and a lump the vet wrongly thought malignant. Last year a rank steer dislocated his hip. One afternoon when I was away on business, Luke slipped out the back door, shed one ewe, and kept her apart from her flock for I don't know how long. During this silent ovine/canine struggle of wills Luke chewed that ewe's ear off. She went into shock and died. Luke is a Blockhead.

Once, several of us were training young sheepdogs when one dog chased a ewe across the Cowpasture River. The sheep clambered up a steep shale cliff onto a four-inch ledge. Luke couldn't get to her from above nor from the left or right, so, with a purity of heart Søren Kierkegaard might have admired, Luke jumped for her, snapping at her wool as he dropped past. I guess he meant to drag her off the ledge into free-fall. Luke missed his grip and hit the river with a mighty sploosh. He is a Blockhead.

I've never done as well with Luke as a better handler might have, but Luke adores me. When I go out at 2 a.m. to check lambing ewes, Luke comes too. When I wake with the night sweats, Luke wakes. He thinks I am a better man than I am. If I sold him, his earnest doggy heart would break.

MOST INTENTIONAL dog-matings are one-night stands. Usually the gyp is brought to the dog and afterwards they never see each other again. Luke and June weren't like that. Mr. and Mrs. Dog have ridden ATVs, flatbed trucks, and rental cars from California to Maine. They've survived car wrecks and they've been body-searched by airline security. Like an old married couple, they hardly seem to notice each other and when June came into heat, they stepped quietly outside into their privacy.

When the puppies were born, June was so fiercely protective no other gyps dared enter the room. Occasionally Luke would amble in and peer into the whelping box, as if he were counting pups. Like many dads, he was uninterested in poop removal.

When Mrs. Dog's pups were three weeks old, she lifted them out of the box. Mr. Dog ambled over, sniffed each pup (*mine!*), and regurgitated his breakfast. Their first solid food. The pups went for Dad's gift like honey.

What Your Dog
Is Trained to Do and Why

And also as touching hounds, men may well help to make them
good by teaching as by leading them to the wood and to fields,
and to always be near them, in making of many good curées
[offal treats] when they have done well, and of ranting at and
beating them when they have done amiss, for they are beasts,
and therefore have they need to learn that what men will they
should do. — Edward of Norwich, 2nd Duke of York

YOUR DOG: what do you want from him? Do you want him to
heel, on and off leash, at your left side? When you say "Come!"
do you want him to race to you, spin, and sit beside you facing
forward? Do you expect him to lie down at a distance? To sit still for five
minutes with you out of the room? Do you expect instant obedience to a
single command?

Chances are, like most dog owners you may want more *don'ts* than *dos*.
Don't poop in the house! *Don't* topple elderly Aunt Hattie with your too
enthusiastic greeting! *Don't* rummage the garbage for edibles! *Don't* surf
the countertop for the Sunday roast! *Don't* attack the neighbors' cat/mini-
poo/pit bull! *Don't* bark so incessantly they call the cops! *Don't* chase cars!
Don't drag me around on the leash! *Don't* tear up the household furniture!

And many, many other *don'ts*, trivial and significant. Strewn garbage is
annoying. The dog who savages a toddler turns lives upside down.

The only positive behavior you probably expect from your dog is coming
when called — coming more or less, and sooner or later. And in fact, many
pet owners are content with dogs that — short of nailing that kid — ignore
the *don'ts* much of the time.

Perhaps you've met dogs that *do* come when called, *do* walk quietly on

29

leash or walk quietly with no leash at all. Perhaps you're considering training your dog. You may seek a trainer at the local big-box pet store or the nearest dog obedience club. Trainers' cards adorn the counter of the seed and feed store or you can google "dog training hometown."

Well, what will you learn and why? Probably you think you already know. You want "obedience."

The lens through which we see our dogs seems self-evident, doesn't it? How else can a dog survive in twenty-first-century-not-particularly-dog-friendly America? Obedient dogs are "good," "civilized," and even more "intelligent" than "disobedient" dogs. Stanley Coren's best-seller *The Intelligence of Dogs* equates a dog breed's genetic IQ with its ability to win AKC obedience trials. Sigh.

If we step back and wipe our lenses, it seems odd that dogs are valued for their ability to "heel," recall to a "front and finish," and "stand for examination," especially since few beloved pet dogs can execute these maneuvers.

I'D ALWAYS ASSUMED the Dog Boy in T. H. White's *The Once and Future King* was a purely literary creation. Not so. As Edward of Norwich wrote in the early fifteenth century:

> The hounds' kennel should be ten fathoms in length and five in breadth, if there be many hounds. And there should be one door in front and one behind, and a fair green, where the sun shineth all day from morning till eve, and that green should be closed about with a paling or with a wall of earth or of stone of the same length and breadth as the hounds' kennel is. And the hinder door of the kennel should always be open so that the hounds may go out to play when they like, for it is a great liking to the hounds when they may go in and out at their pleasure....
>
> I would that some child lie or be in the kennel with the hounds to keep them from fighting.... And also he [the child] should be taught to spin horse hair to make couples for the hounds....
>
> Also I will teach the child to lead out the hounds to scombre twice in the day in the morning and in the evening, so that the sun be up, especially in winter. Then should he let them run and play long in a fair meadow in the sun, and then comb every hound after the other, and wipe them with a

great wisp of straw, and thus he shall do every morning. And then shall he lead them into some fair place.

Such dog boys were the first European dog trainers. If he learned to understand and handle the hounds a boy might be promoted to "varlet," and if he worked hard and was lucky, one day he might become that almost-gentleman, the "huntsman."

Prior to the Industrial Revolution most dogs pulled carts, hunted wolves, deer, and birds, worked livestock, savaged poachers, evaded game-keepers, pulled sleds, retrieved shot ducks, or killed rats, foxes, and badgers.

Pet dogs are a Victorian phenomenon. In *The Animal Estate,* her brilliant analysis of nineteenth-century England's attitudes towards animals, Harriet Ritvo concludes that dog shows (aka "the dog fancy") provided upwardly mobile Victorians with self-affirmation:

> The juxtaposition of arbitrarily established criteria (the major purpose of which was to make judgment possible) with swiftly changing fashions not only in favorite breeds but in preferred types within these breeds symbolized a society where status could reflect individual accomplishments and was, as a result, evanescent, lacking in foundation, and in constant need of reaffirmation. As most dog fanciers were, in this sense, self-created, so their exploitation of the physical malleability of their animals was extremely self-referential. Its goal was to celebrate their desire to manipulate, rather than to produce animals that could be measured by such intrinsic standards as utility, beauty, or vigor.

Or, as one show breeder told me at Westminster, "It's my art. It's like painting with genetics."

Early nineteenth-century American training books were written by bird dog men who were contemptuous of "house dogs." But by 1877, in *Breeding, Training, Management, Diseases &c. of Dogs,* Francis Butler not only taught house dogs the bird dog's "down" (Butler called it the "charge"), but also shaking hands (right and left paws), sitting up, standing up, walking on hind legs, diving under water, jumping through a hoop, playing dead, and "Steady!" with a piece of meat balanced on the dog's nose. To Butler these were tricks, not proofs of obedience.

A little later, S. T. Hammond described a "correction":

Sometimes it is necessary to whip a dog though we think not often. A lecture on the enormity of his sins delivered in a solemn reproachful tone of voice will usually be enough to make the offender so ashamed of himself that he will take great care not to repeat his fault. If it is necessary to whip him use a fine switch, a ladies' riding switch is good, and hit him a few blows with the end of it, blows that will sting and not bruise.

In his *System of Dog Training* (1882), William Sterling taught a dog to beg, walk upright, walk on stilts, carry its tail in its mouth, and other "tricks." He advised, "On those very rare occasions when the whip is necessary, the dog must positively know it has done wrong, and be punished at once."

In 1898, the Humane Education Society of Rhode Island published a two-page dissent, *Man's Faithful Friend,* which proclaimed that "a dog may be taught to do almost anything you would care to have him do, without punishment. Encouragement and petting will produce better results than whipping."

Thus, before that century ended battle lines were drawn for the pet dog trainers' squabbles that flame the internet today.

Dogs were trained to do *tricks* until the Prussians invented *obedience.* Before 1910, military and police dog trainers Colonel Konrad Most and Captain Max von Stephanitz determined which tasks a dog should learn how to do. Consequently, when you take your dog to a pet dog trainer, the trainer will impart skills whose value may be more historic than practical. Not many trainers ask, "Why must my dog 'heel' on the left?"

Er . . . because Prussian officers wore their revolvers on the right?

Most was a brilliant dog man and eighty years after it was published his book has a contemporary feel. Even some "purely positive" trainers admire Most (while quickly deploring his corrections).

The German Shepherds and Dobermann Pinschers Most trained dodged shell fire while delivering orders or bandages. They weren't as submissive as the pet in your lap. While Most cautioned that "erroneous application of compulsion is a deeply rooted evil in training," he also decried ineffectual, nagging corrections: "As in a pack of dogs, the order of hierarchy in a man and dog combination can only be established by physical force, that is by an actual struggle, in which the man is instantly victorious."

Hans Tossutti trained police dogs in Berlin, competed under von Stephanitz, and organized the Potsdam Guide Dogs for the Blind before emigrating to this country, where, in 1928, he established the New England Training School for Dogs. His German Shepherd, Bodo, was a canine movie star. Tossutti introduced several training tools used today: the longe line, the pinch collar, and the throw chain. Although his *Companion Dog Training* has a photo of Bodo climbing a ten-foot ladder into a window, Tossutti didn't train police dogs: "In this country," he wrote, "we want the Companion dog, not the attacker." He praised trainers who refused to undertake "ATTACK-PROTECTION" training (his emphasis).

Tossutti made obedience the foundation for all training. He abjured the dog whip: "For necessary punishment or correction to be effective, we must keep our hands off the dog; moreover, the article used to administer punishment must not be visible. This of course is impossible when a whip is used. While holding a whip in your hand, call a dog to you. Fear of the whip will prompt him to approach you hesitantly, his tail between his legs. And he will not come all the way, but will remain at some distance, out of reach."

Tossutti's invisible correction was the throw chain; when cunningly thrown this light chain startled the dog like a "Bolt from the Blue."

"HUH? Wha dat?! Who done it? Was it something I might have done?" This anonymous correction lets the dog believe his own actions caused the unpleasant effect.

Helene Whitehouse Walker may have studied with Tossutti; certainly she adopted his methods. Mrs. Walker was a wealthy socialite who showed French poodles and hired Blanche Saunders to manage her kennels.

Saunders was an all-round athlete. In high school she competed in swimming, sharpshooting, baseball, basketball, and field hockey. She graduated from Amherst with a major in animal husbandry.

Eventually Saunders would author or coauthor a dozen dog books. Her prose is clear and without affectation. Her "Do's and Don't's" from *Training You to Train Your Dog* remain good advice, six decades after they first appeared:

To accomplish the most in training, certain do's and don't's must be followed. The most helpful of these are:

1. Always play with your dog a few minutes before and after each training period. However, when working, be serious and let your dog know you mean business. Never play and joke with him while you are training. *Never laugh at him.*

2. Do not overtrain. . . .

3. Be consistent. . . .

4. Be patient. . . .

20. See that your dog is in a happy frame of mind at the end of each training period.

Mrs. Walker had been impressed by the working dog tests of the British Associated Sheep, Police, and Army Dog Society (ASPADS). The ASPADS test, although more athletic than modern obedience trials, did test a dog's obedience. In June 1934 she persuaded the North Westchester Kennel Club to offer an obedience test at Mount Kisco, Connecticut.

1. Heel on leash

On the command "heel," the dog should follow as closely as possible to the left knee of the handler. . . . The exercise shall consist of "left turns," "right turns," "about turns," and marching in the "figure eight" at normal walking pace. The judge may at his discretion test also at a fast pace or a very slow pace.

2. Heel free

3. Sit

The dog should sit for the full period of two minutes, handler being out of sight.

4. Recall to handler

The dog should be recalled from the "down" or sitting position, the handler being as far as possible from the dog. While returning the dog should be ordered to stop, which he should do instantly and remain down until called. He should then return at a smart pace and sit in front of the handler. . . .

5. Retrieving a two-pound dumbbell on flat

6. Retrieving 8 to 10 ounce dumbbell over 3 ft. 6 in. standard obstacle

7. Long jump (six feet)

8. Down

> 5 minutes (handlers out of sight). . . . All the dogs in the class should be down together. . . . The judge may cause the dogs to be tested by sending the stewards to walk among them during this exercise.

Mrs. Walker lobbied the American Kennel Club on behalf of obedience trials. She wrote:

> I am more than ever convinced that Obedience Tests can become very popular in this country for many reasons, three in particular:
>
> 1. As an added attraction at dog shows from the spectator point of view, especially the non-doggy one who loves dogs but has no understanding of their points. This should increase the gate, thereby financially helping the show-giving club.
>
> 2. By encouraging *all* breeders to breed for brains and the original purpose of their respective breeds, as well as for show points.
>
> 3. By encouraging the amateur owner of one dog to learn how to train and handle and join in a sport that gives a maximum of pleasure at a minimum of expense.

You may wonder when the part about living happily with your neutered shelter mutt comes in. It doesn't. In 1936, the AKC adopted obedience tests in order to "demonstrate the usefulness of the purebred dog as the companion and guardian of man and not the ability of the dog to acquire facility in the performance of mere tricks."

No mutts need apply.

The price for getting the AKC imprimatur was adding a "stand for examination" exercise to the obedience trial. Although this exercise has limited practical value it is appreciated by show-ring judges who really, really hate getting bit.

Helene Walker, Blanche Saunders, and three standard poodles proceeded to publicize the new dog sport. In their 1936 Buick sedan, towing a twenty-one-foot Auto Cruiser trailer, the indomitable ladies drove from New York to Hollywood via Cincinnati, Wichita, Houston, and Dallas.

Saunders later wrote, "At one stop, Glee (our brilliant obedience worker) delayed things. Spotting a rabbit, she took off in pursuit, ignoring every obedience command in the book. Glee and the rabbit disappeared over the horizon, and that, in Texas, is a long way off."

The ladies survived sandstorms, sand burrs, and biting ants so severe that one dog went into the obedience ring with both eyes swollen shut. Although they packed a pistol they didn't need it, because as Saunders reported, "We had our protection in poodles. When we parked for the night, they became expert at finding hobos asleep under a bush and would chase them with fierce determination." (For less privileged Americans it was the Great Depression.) One southern sheriff worried because no man was traveling with them, and, of course, everybody wanted to know why the poodles looked so funny.

In the end, these spunky ladies established obedience competitions in North America. These competitions were the first and still remain the standard pet dog trainers work toward. The ladies set in concrete the tasks an obedient pet dog could be expected to learn, and when you sign up for a dog training class — whatever method the trainer embraces — your dog will be trained to execute those tasks, invented by Prussian war dog trainers, that Helene Whitehouse Walker and Blanche Saunders refined seventy years ago.

The Trainer's Trainer

I won't refuse to train any dog. — Tony Ancheta

OST DOGS like to be fondled by total strangers about as much as most humans do. But like humans, dogs can be trained to tolerate fondling and some learn to seek it. Every species has its "happy hookers," and before her first literary event I'd hoped June might be such a one.

June had her literary inauguration at eighteen months old when I gave a reading in a southwest Virginia library. While I recited my peerless prose June schmoozed the audience. She was maybe too devoted to her work. June wouldn't give it a rest.

The event organizers had offered to put us up at (a) a motel or (b) a "little farmhouse in the country." I'd pictured an old-timey, slightly run-down, white frame Virginia farmhouse with a lumpy bed for me but lots of outdoors where June could sniff her sniffs and empty.

The simple farmhouse, alas, turned out to be a posh rustic lodge, one of those getaways where businessmen meet to strategize, beat drums, and bond Accounting with Human Resources. Nobody lived in the place. Its owner's hobby, my guide told me, was buying such houses and fixing them up.

"My," I remarked.

The place had been Martha-Stewarted to the nines. Every tchotchke complimented a tchotchke across the room and nothing was in poor or dubious taste. A caribou head hung above the huge stone fireplace where the perfect fire flickered. "Oh," I said stupidly. "The owner hunts."

"Oh no," my guide explained. "He borrowed it."

Meanwhile June, who is reliably housebroken, slipped into the bedroom and chose a perfect white shag carpet for her perfect smelly dump.

So much for my happy hooker.

NOT LONG AFTERWARDS, June and I met Tony Ancheta at a dog train-ers' gathering where Tony was handed an intractable problem. Two Dober-man Pinscher gyps loathed each other. The two battled so ferociously their owner couldn't leave them in the same room. In the car, if their dog crates were near, they'd bloody their gums on the wires trying to get at each other.

Tony is powerfully built and seems bigger than he is. He has an un-nerving capacity for total stillness and his body never says one single thing he doesn't mean. With dogs he is precise and nimble. Imagine a nimble fireplug.

Tony asked for helper dogs and I volunteered June.

Tony stood the more aggressive Doberman on a three-foot-high groom-ing table and waited quietly beside while the volunteer dogs — and her hated rival — paraded by. June hadn't a clue what was going on but trot-ted along like a good sport. Tony lowered the table a notch and asked the helper dogs to pick up the pace.

He lowered the table to ground level. Just once, when the offending Dobie looked as if she just might be considering a move, Tony shouted "Out!" June flinched but kept trotting.

The aggressive Doberman froze. Dog problem? What dog problem? As soon as Tony Ancheta picked up that Doberman's lead, the "intractable" dog problem was solved.

Many dog trainers won't train "aggressive," aka "extremely reactive," dogs — dogs that have attacked humans or other dogs.

Glad you asked why. Suppose you're a pet dog trainer in, say, Duluth. Middle of the night your phone rings and a desperate owner pleads: "Ani-mal control has Spike. They're going to kill Spike!"

Since you've trained dogs for years, here's what you know before you first lay eyes on Spike.

The owner has no idea who Spike is or what Spike needs. He probably believes that for dogs, love conquers all — somehow, sometime. The owner's in denial. This isn't the first time Spike has nailed a human, nor the second time, nor even the third; this is the first time he got caught at it. Spike's human family may be dysfunctional. Probably the family is physically un-healthy, never exercises, and has inconsistent routines.

You, the experienced dog trainer, can probably reform Spike's wicked ways. But what will happen when you return Spike to the environment with the humans who produced those problems? And who gets sued if after you've trained Spike, a day, a month, a year from now, Spike kills or disfigures somebody's kid?

Tony Ancheta accepts those phone calls and dogs like Spike. Every single one of them. He drives to the San Francisco airport, collects the bouncing, snarling dog crate, and brings dog and crate back to his dog yard. His best referrals, Tony jokes, come from animal control.

Tony will train Spike for thirteen weeks, offers a money-back guarantee, and has never had to refund a dime.

His rural California home and training facility is in Gold Rush country three hours east of San Francisco. The summer after his Dobie demonstration June and I walked into Tony's dog yard.

Like most top trainers, Tony has a canine assistant: Damien, a rangy, powerful Doberman Pinscher. Damien makes sure Tony doesn't get blindsided; he disciplines unruly dogs and establishes order in the pack. Although Damien has seen plenty of aggressive dogs, he'd never met a mannerly young gyp like June and June had never imagined a dog like Damien. While Tony trained a Spitz, two Bull Terriers, a Collie mix, and an Elkhound for my instruction, Damien investigated June. June didn't care for his attention but wasn't sure she could object.

Damien wasn't trying to mount or harm June, but he was Dweeb on Four Feet: "Hi, there! Damn you're cute! Anybody ever tell you you're cute? Damn you're cute!" Since it was high time June understood her female prerogatives, I didn't interfere and Tony and I left both dogs loose while we went inside for lunch, during which Tony shared a cheese sandwich with an ancient, flatulent Dachshund mix: "Buster Brown, the bone-eating hound."

When we came back out, June had asserted herself and Damien was properly respectful — to his relief and hers. All sane dogs like to know the rules.

Back in San Francisco late in the afternoon I parked in Chinatown. I wanted to buy a gift for Anne's birthday.

Yes, I should have left June in the car in the parking garage. She and I were two blocks down Grant Avenue before I realized my mistake.

For country dog June, Chinatown wasn't exotic and fascinating: it was Sheepdog Hell. The pedestrians didn't move like the rural Americans she was used to and there were thousands of pedestrians. Some startled when they discovered a black and white dog at their feet. Their body language was — well, it was Chinese to June. When a parade came down the street with cymbals, whistles, firecrackers, and drums, June completely lost it. If she hadn't been leashed, she would have bolted.

A runaway dog in a strange city . . . For my immature gyp, it had been a tough day.

TONY ANCHETA trained his first dog fifty years ago using a book he found in the local library. He so enjoyed the challenge, he trained all the dogs in the neighborhood. "If it wagged," Tony says, "I trained it." When he spotted a dog-training class in the local park, he worked his dog on the periphery until the graduation test. The instructor invited him to give it a try and Tony's dog earned the highest score.

Tony confessed he was a pretty fair dog trainer. Dick Koehler, the instructor, said, "Stop by our kennel tomorrow. Ask for my father, Bill."

For twenty-one years Bill Koehler had trained Disney's motion picture animals. Bill Koehler had authored the library book Tony trained from.

Next morning, when the not-entirely-chastened young trainer arrived at the Koehler home, Bill Koehler told him to expect his first client. Okay. Polite chitchat until a big van rolled into the driveway, its ramp dropped, and a quadriplegic rolled his electric wheelchair down it. He had some movement in one hand and a BIG dog to train.

Which was the very moment Tony Ancheta turned pro.

Tony worked with Bill and Dick Koehler for years, and after his mentors passed on, he inherited the Koehler school and method.

Bill Koehler's famous/notorious *The Koehler Method of Dog Training* distilled a lifetime's training experience, is one of the best-selling training books of all time, and was profoundly influential with a generation of professional dog trainers, some of whom are still training today. A few real dopes misused Koehler techniques intended for mankillers by applying them to harmless family pets.

In his book's introduction, Bill Koehler wrote:

> The book's methods are applicable to those dogs that resist training, as well as to the tractable dogs, which are in the great majority.
>
> Thought by thought and act by act the objective of this book is to enable the reader to train the dog he now has, regardless of its conduct and character, to a point where he and his dog will enjoy the fullest companionship....

Bill Koehler made a big promise: although you may have never trained a dog, if you start with chapter 1, do each exercise as described, and practice as specified you will produce an obedient dog regardless of the dog's breed characteristics, individual aptitude (or lack thereof), or prior life experiences.

Soft-spoken in person, Bill Koehler wrote scrappy prose. His wrath was triggered by ineffective training methods and those he described as "whiners," "naggers," and "humaniacs." Bill Koehler had an unfortunate knack for invective.

A savvier editor would have warned that describing extreme corrections for dangerous dogs was inappropriate in a text designed for inexperienced pet owners training mild family pets.

> Since we are presently concerned with the dog that bites in resentment of the demands of training, we will set our example in that situation....
>
> First, the trainer makes certain that the collar and leash are more than adequate for any jerk or strain that the dog's most frantic actions could cause. Then he starts to work the dog deliberately and fairly to the point where the dog makes his grab. Before the teeth have reached their target, the dog, weight permitting, is jerked from the ground. As in coping with some of the aforementioned problems, the dog is suspended in midair.
>
> **However, to let the biting dog recover his footing while he still had strength to renew the attack would be a cruelty** [Koehler's emphasis]. The only justifiable course is to hold him suspended until he has neither the strength nor inclination to renew the fight.
>
> When finally it is obvious that he is physically incapable of expressing his resentment and is lowered to the ground, he will probably stagger looplegged for a few steps, vomit once or twice, and roll over on his side.

The sight of a dog lying thick-tongued on his side is not pleasant, but do not let it alarm you.

In 1986, when an interviewer asked Koehler why he was so angry, he said it was a preemptive strike. "See, I think most people are sane, and I wanted a way that I could alienate all the nuts and get the mentally sound people to read my book.... I guess the nicest thing that can happen to you is to enjoy the enmity of the incompetent." For good measure, he added: "These humaniacs are the worst damned enemies that dogs and other people have.... A lot of this stuff sounds so nice — 'WE LOVE our doggies.' Cripe. They don't really love 'em, they love themselves, and they love their image of being such kind people. And I'll tell you this, when their dog gets killed unnecessarily from running out in traffic, they're very apt to go the whole route and put a little box edged in black in Off-lead magazine or one of those: 'Ferdie, 1979–1982.' And the poor dog would be alive today if they had vertebras instead of Jello."

By mixing advanced and beginner techniques, and by being contentious (if you don't like him) or too honest (if you do), Bill offered his "humaniac" adversaries a big, fat target.

Did they take advantage of that? Bet your booties they did.

FOUR YEARS and a litter of pups after we visited Tony Ancheta, June was trying to get qualified for the World Trials and I was looking for a few good epiphanies, so we sat in on Tony's "Correctly Koehler" seminar at a high-end horse and dog training center in Moorestown, New Jersey.

Although Tony hates ineffective dog training as much as Bill Koehler did, Tony is no ranter. He's less confrontational than his mentor and doesn't mention the most controversial Koehler corrections — not because these corrections are *never* necessary but because they are so *rarely* necessary.

Shrugging off Koehler critics, Tony says, "Koehler method has been training dogs successfully for sixty years. When you're *numero uno,* everybody's shooting arrows at you."

It was a nice spring morning, but twenty trainers and our dogs were inside a prefab steel building: fluorescent lights, rubber mats on the floor (better traction for the dogs), dog crates against one wall, and metal folding chairs. Tony's taught hundreds of classes and drilled ideas in his pupils' minds:

"How long is the dog confined before training?"

"Four hours," we reply dutifully.

"How long without food?" Tony cups an ear.

"Four hours."

"Without water?"

"One hour."

THE KOEHLER METHOD'S greatest innovation is teaching your dog to pay attention to you.

"Huh?" you may respond. "All I need to get Spike's attention is a treat."

What if you haven't got one? What if Spike isn't hungry? What if he's more interested in the gyp whose scent is wafting across a busy street?

Bill Koehler wanted and now Tony Ancheta wants Spike's attention on YOU.

Unfortunately, that's trickier than it sounds because — if the truth be told — you're probably unworthy of your dog's attention.

Let me back up. Remember that incident between Tony and the aggressive Doberman? I'll bet you thought I was just woofling when I wrote that the dog was under Tony's control the same instant Tony picked up the leash? That was no poetic exaggeration, it was fact. But it sure as hell wouldn't have happened if you or another civilian had picked up that Doberman's leash.

Every dog's primary language is body language. If dogs had a Shakespeare, he'd be Nureyev. Dogs accurately read attitude, intent, health, and state of mind at a great distance — not merely other dogs' but humans' too. Prehistoric dogs who couldn't read humans did not survive to breed.

Problem is: we're not Nureyevs. In dog terms, we're not even Gomer Pyle. We humans take vital cues from accent, grooming, and attire, and our pack leaders may be physically incoherent — Richard Nixon and George W. Bush have occupied the highest office in the land. But klutzes cannot train dogs, because to the dog, their body language is gibberish.

Right about now, you may be thinking, "My poor dog—I can't even dance the tango."

Although dog-lucid body language can be learned, it takes years, and since you aren't likely to learn your dog's language, the dog must learn about you. That's the genius of the Koehler method—the trainer doesn't train the dog, the trainer sets up situations where the dog trains the dog.

And the very first step, the necessary step, is longe line work.

Vicki Hearne described how it works in *Adam's Task:*

> I take her out of her kennels and am silent except for a calm, "Good morning Salty." I put her on a fifteen-foot line, attached to a training collar, and I begin to go for a little walk. Salty stays at my side for about one and one-quarter seconds, which is how long it takes her to spot something huntable—in this case, my motley colored cat, Touchstone. . . . Salty heads for Touchstone at proper field-trial speed. I say nothing to her—nothing at all. . . . I drop all fifteen foot of slack into the line and turn and run in the opposite direction, touchdown style. Salty hits the end of the line and travels, perforce, some distance in the direction I am going, tumbling end-over end. . . .
>
> The third or fourth time she gets dumped in this way, it dawns on Salty that there is a consistency in my inconsiderate and apparently heedless plunges. She sits down in order to think this over, cocking her head in puzzlement, trying to work out the implications of my behavior.
>
> By the end of the first session she is more attentive to me, more willing to try and follow—to try, that is, to understand—than she has ever been to anyone in the whole course of her life, and I've said *nothing* to her.

The longe line gets Salty's attention *despite* the human's inadequate body language. Klutzes can train with a longe line. Quadriplegics in electric wheelchairs can use it. You *can* get your dog attending to you.

If the dog sulks, walk on. If the dog whimpers, walk on. If the dog lies flat, drag him. It's the dog's job to be attentive to you—not you to the dog.

Tony Ancheta says you shouldn't talk to Salty for the first six days of longe line training. Not even celebrations after a successful lesson. Tony grins. "After six days you can relax and become an idiot again."

Those who had signed up for Tony's "Correctly Koehler" seminar were professional trainers there to refresh their understanding of the foundational traditional training method.

Most of their dogs were AKC purebreds, but there were rescue mutts, too. Vivian Bregman's charming Border Collie Goniff had earned an OTCH title — Obedience Trial Champion. Outdoors on breaks, the dogs were mannerly, quiet, and attentive to their owners. All but Goniff and June were on lead.

In two days, Tony Ancheta summarized the thirteen-week basic Koehler training program. It kept him talking. He demonstrated every physical move and, dutifully, we repeated his training koans.

"The first rule about a throw chain is?"

"The dog can't see you throw it."

"The second rule about a throw chain is?"

"You must hit the dog."

Week one is devoted to the longe line; week two, heeling and sitting; week three, sit-stay and stand. Counterintuitively, the dog doesn't learn to come until week four.

After sixty years of refinement, the Koehler method is meticulous. Tony designated proper throw chain gauges for big and little dogs (eighteen links of no. 2/0 twisted link machine chain for a fifty-pound dog), and suggested strategies if the hardware store clerk is reluctant to cut the chain to the correct length ("That's a very small purchase, sir").

During the lunch break, June decided to say hello to a fluffy white gyp whose owner shrieked, "She's in heat!"

I said, "June's a female."

The woman reeled in her pet. "She should be on a leash! Get her away from us."

I called the puzzled June to my side.

With thirteen weeks of training to condense and explain, Tony and his volunteers demonstrated each precisely choreographed move. By day's end, June was bored and my mind was spinning.

The next morning, Tony explained how to prepare a dog for the AKC CD test. The Companion Dog title is awarded to dogs that can heel on and off leash, stand for examination, sit for one minute, down for three minutes, and recall. Demonstrating the exercises, volunteers marched to and fro on the rubber mats, looking—I thought—very much like Prussian officers out of uniform.

As the clinic wound down a trainer mentioned a too common problem: most owners haven't the patience or free time for a thirteen-week dog training class. These days, most beginning training classes are only six weeks. Tony assured us: if a student doesn't complete the thirteen-week Koehler course, they can pick it up where they left off at a later date.

June was snoozing behind my chair while Goniff lolled at Tony's feet. As he answered our questions, Tony stroked Goniff's head. I don't think he noticed what he was doing. Dogs are a constant in Tony Ancheta's life. There's always a dog under his hands.

A Desperate Gamble

L IKE WILLIAM BLAKE'S *Songs of Innocence,* the appeal of sheepdog trialing is simplicity: nothing exists outside your run. Debts, sins, bad health, marital difficulties, all those insults life so willingly provides: disappeared. Donald's ego dies into the intricate, fluid man/dog/ sheep task. Trialing is serial immortalities; each run, eternity in an hour.

Alas, there's nothing simple about simplicity.

The National Finals Sheepdog Trials is the North American sheepdog Super Bowl. The trial rotates between the East Coast, Midwest, and West Coast, on different fields, under different conditions, with fresh (undogged) sheep. Sheepdog trials are both sport and genetic strategy. Countless farm and ranch dogs in dozens of countries descend from dogs proven at sheepdog trials.

Moving the Finals to a different venue annually is difficult for a volunteer organization, and a couple years back, sheepdoggers considered buying property for the Finals somewhere in the Midwest. Grandstands and parking for handlers and spectators would be permanent and the spectator base would grow. Trials that stay put — like the ones held in Kingston, Ontario; Meeker, Colorado; and Soldier Hollow, Utah — draw tens of thousands of spectators.

I favored a permanent location until I asked Alasdair MacRae, who has won the Finals twelve times, for his thinking. "Dogs run differently on different fields," Alasdair replied.

Bingo! There are fields where my dogs usually do well and fields where the Mister and Missus can't set a paw right. If the National Finals were in the same field every year, we'd all breed to dogs that did well in that single venue and inevitably we'd narrow the sheepdog gene pool, losing dogs that might be toppers on other fields or on other sheep. A fixed venue would have benefitted the trialing *sport* but not trialing's genetic purpose. So we didn't do it.

Qualifying for the Finals is straightforward. The top 20 percent of dogs in any sanctioned open trial earn points. If 50 dogs run, first place earns 10 points, tenth gets 1. As of August 1, the 150 dogs with the most points are qualified to compete in that year's Finals. The $200 entry fee isn't prohibitive — the real cost is two weeks off work plus travel. Finals prize money is negligible: only the top three dogs will earn enough to cover expenses. If you live in California, you'd best be confident you're going to win something before you load up Spot and cross country to this year's Finals in Gettysburg, Pennsylvania. Not every owner of a qualified dog makes the sacrifice.

I'd calculated it would take 25 points to get in. As the August 1 deadline approached, June had 33 points, but Luke had 11.6. Although the Gettysburg Finals weren't far from the farm, I planned to skip this year. I don't like entering a trial with one dog. Sheepdog trials demand everything the dog has to give and a bit more. Dogs that can work all day on farm or ranch are utterly spent after fifteen minutes on a trial course. Focus matters. Focus hurts.

Cool as a cuke I'm not, and if I'm running only one dog, I ask too much of him, heaping Donald stress atop trial stress. Naturally I appreciate your advice: "Chill out," "Act like you don't care."

Gosh, what swell ideas!

Sometimes my dog deserves a better man than I am.

My dog Harry ran brilliantly at the 1994 Finals and afterwards Cheryl Williams, who was an emergency room nurse in her day job, congratulated me. "But," she added, "I was afraid you'd pass out in the shedding ring, you were hyperventilating so bad."

I did notice my vision dimming and getting blurry at the edges but so long as I could see Harry and the sheep . . .

Unfortunately, the USBCHA waited until July before announcing how handlers would be picked for the United States Team competing in the World Trials in South Wales the following October. There were several paths to qualification, but my only shot was doing very well at Gettysburg, the qualifying deadline of which was two weeks away.

The dogs and I had spent thousands of hours training, traveling, and trialing. I'd sat at the feet of top sheepdog and pet dog trainers with my ears open and mouth shut. At seven years going on eight, Luke and June were in their prime. I'd be sixty-eight next year. If not now, when?

Before the August 1 cutoff date, there was only one more qualifying trial in the southeast, Dr. Ben Ousley's outside Lawndale, North Carolina. Crunch time: Luke had to earn enough points at Dr. Ben's to qualify for Gettysburg. Then, we'd need to do well at the National Finals to qualify for the World Trials. Then . . . I'd worry about "then" later.

IT WAS NOT the best time to go away. Zippy, my wife's beloved fourteen-year-old gyp, was dying. Anne was caring for a neighbor's two Cocker Spaniels so our six-dog pack had become eight. Puppy Slick had torn a pad and June had a smelly vaginal discharge. Oh yeah, the electrician was coming to install new service boxes.

Anne and I have been together forty years. She has put up with a lot.

I offered a compromise: I'd take four of the eight dogs to North Carolina where Dr. Ben could check Slick's pad and June's vaginal discharge. If Zippy died I'd quit the trial and come straight home.

As I recall, Anne said, in so many words, "I'll get you for this."

So Friday I drove six hours to Lawndale, North Carolina, where Dr. Ben patched Slick's pad, diagnosed June's pyometra, and put her on an antibiotic. Dr. Ben is mild and thoughtful. "June's temperature is normal and she's showing no signs of distress so you can run her. But pyometra is serious and you should have her spayed as soon as you get home."

It was unusually tough competition for a benefit trial with no prize money or ribbons. Handlers from Pennsylvania, Florida, and Alabama had come to put a few more qualifying points on their dogs. Six of the entrants had made the top twenty at previous National Finals and I figured twenty of the sixty dogs entered were good enough to win. Most just needed a point or two to put them over the magic 25, Luke needed 14.

When I called home, Zip was still alive, and Anne held the phone against her dog's ear so I could wish Zip well in this life and the next.

Luke ran early in the cool of the day and his run was impeccable. When we reached the shedding ring I glanced at my watch: three minutes left, plenty of time. Luke's a brilliant shedder, but he's nervy and if he panics, he'll grip (bite) a sheep — disqualified, score: zero. The ewes were trial-savvy Katahdins who knew perfectly well what Luke and I intended and they didn't wanna. They swirled, they clung together like velcro, and when I checked my watch again, we had fifty seconds to complete both shed and pen.

In for a penny. I spotted a six-inch gap and called Luke through and though Luke wanted to bite, my shout brought him to his senses. He re-gathered his sheep as I jogged to the pen and jerked the gate open. These Katahdins didn't like an assertive dog at the pen so I downed Luke, penned them myself, and banged the gate shut as my timer started beeping.

I've chronic bronchitis and as I gasped and coughed off the course I wished I'd remembered to take my meds. Exhausted, Luke wallowed in the tub of cool water.

When the trial was all over, Luke had second place with 10.8 qualifying points. His new total was 22.4 — just a few precious points shy of what I figured he'd need. I entered both dogs — just in case.

THIRTEEN YEARS AGO, Anne was grieving when puppy Zippy climbed onto her lap and licked the tears from her cheeks. Zippy was never a useful sheepdog but for fourteen years she was a very good dog. She lived three more days after I got home.

Though June seemed fine, when our vet opened her, her inflamed, grossly swollen uterus was stuffed with putrid bacteria and ready to burst. My desperate gamble was more desperate than I'd thought. I might have killed June.

Some handlers with higher scores than Luke's didn't enter the Gettys-burg Finals; other high-scorers canceled. By mid-August the cutoff score had dropped from 28 to 22.6. On Monday, August 27, only four dogs were ahead of Luke, but after September 1, there'd be no others accepted no mat-ter how many more dropped out. If we were in September 1, we'd be in; if out, out.

At 3 p.m., August 31, Francis Raley phoned to tell me Luke was in. Last dog in the 150.

The E-collar

Most pet owners would be appalled to know how austere
their dog's world really is. — Behesha Doan

I N T H E S E C O N D G R A D E, I was introduced to addition, subtraction,
and basic multiplication. The teacher taught with flashcards. She'd
hold up a card:

$$5$$
$$+$$
$$6$$
$$=?$$

and ask some unfortunate student to supply the answer. I stuttered my best
guess: "Uh? Fifty-six?"

Whereupon the teacher would flip the card to reveal the answer I'd
failed to compute. "Yes, Donald. Five plus six equals eleven. You really
must try harder."

The harder I tried, the fewer correct answers I got. My wild guesses pro-
voked giggles from girls who got the right answer every time.

Then I made a life-altering discovery: the flashcards were translucent! I
took a seat in the front of the room, which the teacher approved, thinking
it marked an attitude change. In truth, my front row seat put the big, bright
windows behind her so I could read the answer through the flashcard.

Subsequently, my mathematical abilities varied with the weather. Sullen,
overcast days: I was hopeless. On sunny days I was Kurt Godel.

Today, my mathematical skills are negligible, but I am an excellent backwards reader. If you're filling out a contract on your side of the desk, I can
read it upside down as well as you can right side up.

The danger with electric training collars is teaching, powerfully, what
you do not intend to teach. I'll call these devices "e-collars" because that's

what their practitioners prefer. We sheepdoggers call them shock collars and don't use them much.

I saw my first e-collar-trained sheepdog at a Canadian trial in the early nineties. The dog had been imported and the Scottish trial judge knew him before he crossed the water. The dog began a nice outrun but a hundred yards out he lurched and spun around before proceeding hesitantly toward his sheep. I was near enough to hear the judge gasp, "My God! What have you done to him!"

My guess: the sheepdog, whose verbal or body language corrections had previously come from his handler, had been outrunning during training and made a mistake — perhaps he'd crossed instead of going behind the sheep — and his handler had shocked hell out of him.

So what did that dog learn? He certainly didn't learn that his handler was displeased with something he was doing. He didn't learn to shun crossovers. The dog was hit with a Bolt from the Blue and left to interpret the message for himself. Maybe he decided to avoid sagebrush (the brush he'd been near). Maybe he learned that certain shadows might hurt him. Maybe he learned a sagey smell in his nostrils meant he was about to be shocked. Like me with the flashcards, that dog took the wrong lesson from his experience.

For a time, some very good sheepdog handlers experimented with e-collars. Many fine dogs were ruined for sheepwork and sold for a pittance to be retrained to chase geese off golf courses.

Working Border Collie magazine is deliberately uncontroversial, but one month it was devoted to top trainers arguing against shock collars. They've become rare in sheepdog culture. E-collar use — or dummy e-collar use — is forbidden at USBCHA-sanctioned sheepdog trials.

I didn't give e-collars another thought until I needed one. Our farm lies between 186,000 acres of uninhabited national forest and 36,000 acres of State Game Commission land. My neighbors routinely freeze or can half a dozen deer a year and the Highland County high school is closed on opening day of rifle season so sons can hunt with their dads. Unfortunately, not every bullet produces a clean kill and wounded deer come to brush along the river to die. One year I counted twelve deer carcasses on our farm.

Crack of dawn I let our dogs out while I get dressed, stoke the fire, and put the coffeepot on. Out means *out:* they wander as they will, and over the years we've grown accustomed to them bringing unseemly, unidentifiable deer parts home. What carrion the sheepdogs don't find, our sheep-guarding dogs do.

Except for the unpleasant aesthetics and being awakened by the sound and subsequent smell of a dog vomiting beside my bed, this hadn't been a problem until three years ago when a new strain of botulism appeared in the county. Botulism is a neurotoxin produced by the bacteria *Clostridium botulinum,* which thrives in carrion. Dogs are supposed to be immune to it, but mine sure weren't.

Botulism paralyzes muscles. In our dogs, the first symptom was wobbly hindquarters. When poor June tried to jump off the bed, she splayed and hit the floor flat. If the dog has ingested enough toxin, it paralyzes the lungs and the dog suffocates.

There really wasn't much we could do. If a dog was outdoors suspiciously long or came in licking his lips, we induced vomiting, but three times that fall I drove to the emergency vet with a dog I had to carry into the clinic.

There wasn't much the vet could do either; our emergency clinic doesn't have a ventilator. The vet confirmed my diagnosis, kept my dog hydrated until the toxin left his system, and produced a bill. Luke's dormant Lyme disease was reactivated by the botulism. At 2 a.m., Luke was whimpering in excruciating pain as I toted him to the car for the hour-long race to the vet clinic. Luke's tab was $1,000.

While I could call my dogs off carrion, there wasn't much I could do after dark or when they slipped off into the tuckerbrush. I couldn't let them out without monitoring, and I couldn't walk them anywhere they might find carrion, which was pretty much everywhere.

I'd seen pet dog trainer George Cockrell demonstrate the e-collar so I asked him for help. George suggested I modify Bill Koehler's poison-proofing method for guard and patrol dogs who were taught that food outside their bowls was bad, bad, bad.

George gave me an e-collar and transmitter. After four days, June didn't notice the collar and wouldn't associate me with the correction. I drove down a logging road where I routinely walked the dogs and marked the carrion drop.

Then a friend donned surgical gloves (no human scent on the bait) and dropped offal at my mark.

An hour later, June walked ahead off lead. She raised her nose to sniff, ran to the bait, and as her nose touched the offal I zapped her — six on a scale of nine. June screamed. One treatment cured her. Blockhead Luke needed two. But for weeks afterwards he would only eat out of my hand. Luke thought *all* food might be dangerous, and for eighteen months he would accept a bone from my hand but wouldn't pick it up if I tossed it to him.

Three years after their inoculation, Luke and June would probably gobble carrion again. Fortunately, the lethal botulism strain has vanished, but we keep ipecac and an e-collar on hand in case it reappears.

ENGINEER AND HUNTER Frank Hoover invented the shock collar in 1962. He never told Bill Boatman, his eventual business partner, exactly what he did when he worked at Los Alamos. Hoover was a hound man and like all hound men, he wanted to break his dogs of running trash ("trash" is defined as any critter he wasn't hunting). Before Hoover invented the shock collar the standard remedy for a dog running trash was the "#9 correction"— i.e., number nine shot, three hundred yards, open choke. More than a few hounds were blinded by that correction.

Frank Hoover's eureka moment came one fine summer afternoon when he saw a kid flying a radio-controlled model airplane. His prototype was a crude aluminum box riveted to the collar. Hoover hand-assembled them and sold them through coon dog and beagle magazines. Bill Boatman, who was running a hunter's supply store, saw the ads, traveled to New Mexico, and bought the business. "Frank's was a kitchen table on the back porch operation," Boatman jokes. "I turned it into a garage operation."

Boatman's improved unit was fiberglass over wire mesh and came in three models: quarter-mile, half-mile, and three-quarter-mile. The three-quarter-mile model sold for $299. If a collar couldn't shock beyond a quarter mile it was $99.

Today, a two-mile unit costs $199.

Other manufacturers copied the basic design and sold them, euphemistically, as "electronic training collars" or "remote collars." The first retrievers trained by an e-collar were robodogs that didn't go out with any force. But after the variable intensity collar was invented trainers' methods improved, and today almost all field-trial bird dogs and retrievers are e-collar trained.

In the late eighties, Innotek designed compact collars that could be used on much smaller dogs and e-collars entered the pet market. Innotek was bought by Radio Systems Corporation, which also manufactures underground electric dog fences. Once underground electric fences won acceptance in suburbia, consumers started buying e-collars to train their pets.

Although Bill Boatman no longer manufacturers the collars he sells, he keeps a close eye on the market. He estimates $70 to $78 million worth of hunting dog e-collars are sold every year. "The pet dog market must be three times that," Bill says.

BEHESHA DOAN is licensed by the Drug Enforcement Administration and the Illinois Law Enforcement Training and Standards Board for remote collar training and police K-9 unit tactical operations. She's on the training advisory board of the International Association of Canine Professionals (IACP) and narrates TriTronics's e-collar instructional DVD. Her specialties are tracking, man-trailing, and police K-9 work. She's articulate, precise, and modest in a profession where modesty is rare.

Doan's Illinois training facility is in the northern tip of the Ozarks, south of the Crab Orchard National Wildlife Refuge. It's farm country and her end-of-the-road facility is shaded by pine and hickory trees.

Luke, June, and I paused there en route to an Indiana sheepdog trial at one of those Scottish festivals where clans whose ancestors murdered each other celebrate the good old days. After eleven hours, the dogs were glad to be out of the car. They stretched, they sniffed, they did their business. The sky was overcast and storms were predicted. June hates thunderstorms, Luke tolerates them.

Behesha's e-collar seminar was in a big metal building with the familiar rubber mats on the floor. Most students were police officers. Two in neat blue jackets were instructors from the ATF dog training facility in Front Royal, Virginia.

So much copness made me faintly uneasy.

I GUESS I EXPECTED Behesha to slap an e-collar on a dog straightaway, but she began with slides of wolves interacting.

"Attempting to learn to use any training tool without some understanding or guidance in how dogs interact, learn, and relate makes the tool user little more than a technician. Training requires that we come to understand that there is an entirely different language, behavior, and value system that exists in the dogs we are teaching than what we as humans experience."

Behesha asked her students (me too) to read canine language in the slides she projected. She smiled. "The first thing the dog says every morning, as soon as he gets up, is 'What's different today?'"

Behesha and Mary McCarthy, her assistant, worked like team preachers, reinforcing and amplifying each other's remarks.

"The dog's need for leadership is a deep, persistent desire for reassurance born of structure and connection with its pack. When this need is satisfied, dogs experience confidence, security, strength, and stability. This permits their bonds to expand, and a sense of fundamental cooperation is present in their attitudes."

As Behesha taught, ripe hickory nuts banged onto the metal roof of the building. It was like being inside a steel drum.

After several hours improving our dog reading skills, we broke and I let Luke and June out while Behesha leashed a rescue German Shepherd. I was grateful for that leash. Luke and June are first-rate dog readers and they gave that Shepherd a wide berth. Like too many German Shepherds, this dog's hindquarters were so low it seemed to be lunging when it was standing still. Dog show breeders have created a dog so malformed it cannot walk without pain. That dog's pain might explain my dogs' wariness.

Back in the steel drum building, we examined more wolf photographs, peppered with Behesha's probing questions. If we didn't understand this language, she insisted, if we didn't know what the dog was saying, we couldn't train it.

Behesha's modesty and candor are appealing. In an email, she wrote:

> I am less a Trainer than my dog is a Learner. This lesson was brought home to me more than a decade ago when I was face to face with a particularly difficult dog named Lando. Lando and I worked together for months, and I used every tool in the proverbial toolbox to find the mix that made sense to him. Yet, week after week, his cooperation/aggression seemed to appear spontaneously, and without announcement. Nothing made sense according to all I had learned about dogs. I came to realize that there was only one of two things I could do: send the dog down the road with some "no guarantees" type stipulation, or recognize that I had far more to learn than Lando did, and that maybe, for a while, I should wear the hat of a student rather than a trainer.
>
> That was a powerful, intuitive time for me and it became a turning point in my career when I came to realize that I could help Lando more if I stopped sifting his actions through the theoretical framework from which I was taught . . . That meant that I had to stop trying to be like, think like, and act like all the trainers I had sought so hard to emulate. I would have to have total confidence that this dog wanted to communicate with me, and I had to have confidence in my ability to hear him.

Mary McCarthy's Golden Retriever Robin will, on command, pick up a quarter and deliver it to her owner. Dogs hate to bite metal and a quarter is thin and difficult to tooth off a floor. Despite Robin's extraordinary training, like all the other dogs on break, Robin was on leash. Mary told me, "I always have the e-collar on so I can always mean what I say."

At the end of the day, Behesha's students and I had a convivial dinner at a nearby steakhouse and Luke and June had convivial steak dinner scraps later in the motel. I can direct you to good steakhouses near every major sheepdog trial in this country and Canada.

The next day, rain was predicted and I'd need to leave early. When I arrived at her training building, Behesha was letting her dogs out. "Good morning, my son," she crooned to each. "Good morning."

Notebooks at the ready and coffee cups balanced on our knees, we attended when Behesha introduced Nile, a young Labrador Retriever, to the e-collar. He waited on a long, loose lead while she carefully adjusted the "stim" or "tick," going up the dial until Nile reacted. He frowned. He scratched an itch. Then, without using the leash, Behesha "tapped" the dog until he found refuge, attentive and quiet at her side.

"The first thing I want you to notice is the countenance of the dog," Behesha noted. "If you use leash pops, you see the head go down, the tail goes down, and the dog is abashed. You're not seeing any of this with the collar. The key is he's learned the lesson that was meant."

Nile showed no sign of distress. On the contrary; instead of worried unsettled motion, he became a calm member of the pack.

Since Nile was being trained as a search dog, his second lesson was the "go out." Mary McCarthy offered treats twenty feet ahead of Nile while Behesha "tapped" him. Within five minutes Nile was going out on command. (Unlike the hickory nuts thudding onto the metal roof the "taps" are soundless.) Behesha observed, "We use the collar to tap into what is natural to the dog. People feel that we're 'miracle workers' for getting a dog to do what it has never done before in his whole life because the owners can't hear what we're doing."

When sheets of rain joined the hickory nuts I crated June and Luke in the car. They hate storms and crates offer some relief.

At the next break, an ATF officer shared his vision of what an ideal search dog could do. This uberdog could pick out a suicide bomber in the departure terminal at LAX and, without spooking the bomber, identify him to the dog's handler. Since consequences for the bomber would be dire (google: Jean Menezes), the dog had to be 100 percent correct.

One hundred percent. Now there's a vision!

Luke and June have far more latitude. I can usually afford one wrong command, instantly corrected, and still get around a trial course. We can recover from their slight error — refusing a command, beginning to come in too tight, even June's "bumping" the sheep — and still place.

I guess I'm looking for, oh . . . 95 percent.

While we were eating lunch, Behesha got an upsetting phone call. A Chicago newspaper reported that gangbangers were using e-collars to shock their fighting dogs, and some busybody called to accuse Behesha of selling shock collars to abusive thugs.

"In the first place," she told her caller, "I don't sell e-collars. And in the second place, nobody who comes to me uses one until they have been thoroughly trained by me and my staff."

She emailed me: "The moment a person can open their mind to the concept that there are things about remote collars and remote collar training that they do not yet know, is the moment I can have a dialogue with them. Prior to that point, as a trainer in their eyes I am defined by my tool, which is always limited to their own negative experience or ignorance."

The rain quit and Luke, June, and I had miles to go before we slept. I wished I could stay longer. I have seen different dogs, different breeds, and different trainability exposed to e-collar training. These dogs were not abused and, as important, they were not CONFUSED.

I thanked Behesha for letting me sit in. I told her, "The e-collar's a powerful tool."

"Yes."

"I just wish any dog-ignorant civilian couldn't buy one on a whim at PetSmart."

"I wish that too," Behesha Doan said.

Mrs. Dog Buys Our Ticket

━━━━━━━━━━━━━━

THE NATIONAL FINALS Sheepdog Trials began at noon on Tuesday, September 18, in a forty-acre field outside Gettysburg, Pennsylvania. One hundred fifty dogs would be winnowed to forty, who'd then compete in the semifinals Saturday. The best seventeen of those would run on Sunday for the championship. If Luke or June reached that magical top seventeen, we'd be on the United States Team to compete in the World Trials. If either Mister or Missus got into the semifinals, we still had a shot.

The outrun was 470 yards across a rumpled field with a deep gully after the lift (the moment of first dog/sheep contact), so sheep and dog dropped out of sight for what seemed like forever but probably wasn't more than twenty seconds. In that gully, the sheep might veer left or right and often reappeared wildly off the correct line to a "dogleg" post 300 yards in front of the handler.

Earlier that summer, our trial field had hosted Civil War reenactors, who'd erected a low rock wall behind which blue could repel gray or vice versa. A straight fetch would bring sheep and dog over that wall. Should a dog snag its paw under a loose rock, its owner might have a $500 cruciate ligament operation and a dog laid up for weeks.

Hence the dogleg fetch. The dog should lift his sheep and fetch them a hundred yards or so where all vanished into that gully. The sheep would reappear (one hoped) at the dogleg post, after which they'd turn forty degrees toward the fetch panels at the left end of the stone wall.

If you sent your dog left, he'd outrun uphill, through a swale where he couldn't see the waiting sheep or his anxious handler. Three hundred yards out he'd disappear into that gully and Lord knows where he'd come up. If he emerged where he ought, he'd enter dense woods. Through the woods, for the first time since leaving his handler, the dog could see the sheep. During the left outrun, the handler would lose sight of his dog until it got to the sheep.

Sending right seemed the smarter option.

I CAN'T PUT IT OFF any longer. Here's everything you wanted to know — and more — about sheepdog trials.

There are simpler doggy tests, tests most dogs easily pass, viz., the AKC's "herding" trials. Such faux trials gratify owners who can win prizes and put "herding titles" on their dogs. But the traditional sheepdog trial is not meant to gratify dog owners. The trial is designed to produce useful sheepdogs. Since trials began, the winners' offspring have become working farm and ranch sheepdogs all over the world. Farmers and ranchers don't have time to train dogs, and trust that Sheepdog Shep will "get it" if they yell at him just a little louder. The miracle is: more often than not, Shep does get it.

In 2001, 2002, and 2003, not one sheepdog completed the course at the National Finals. The winner lost the fewest points before he ran out of time. Dog fancy friends are puzzled: "What kind of sport is that?" A Daytona 500 that no stockcar finishes? A Super Bowl without touchdowns or field goals?

Fair enough: what kind of a sport is this?

In 2001, 2002, and 2003, somewhere on a farm, ranch, or remote sheep station, there was a sheepdog that *could* have completed those Finals courses. Sheepdoggers defer to the perfect (visionary) sheepdog. When judging, they leave room on the score sheet — in case the perfect sheepdog appears. In thirty years I know of one (1) perfect score at a sheepdog trial, and everyone — including the handler who earned it — thought the judge had been too generous.

Terrain varies, sheep vary, and no two trials are identical. The most difficult trials are the most popular. During his run, each competing dog must solve unique problems. He may draw bad sheep, or he may run late in the day when it's hot and the sheep are cranky. It may rain or sleet or snow during his run, or a high wind may panic the sheep and deafen the dog. The field may develop "dead spots" where the dog cannot hear his handler's commands.

The Fosterfields trial outside Morristown, New Jersey, bordered Mendham Road. If you ran in the morning, your dog could hear your whisper; but by late afternoon when traffic was bumper-to-bumper on the road, your dog went deaf a hundred yards from your feet.

Fair? No. But if you were a shepherd which dog would you want — the dog that finishes his work despite daunting challenges or the dog that only works near at hand on docile sheep in perfect weather?

Depending on topography (and the host's whim) a given trial might have a right-hand drive, a left-hand drive, a pull-back through the drive panels, or the dog might be asked to drive the fetch panels. Trial hosts omit or modify tasks — either because no dog could accomplish the task without harming itself or the stock or because a task is too easy.

North America has a few arena trials: timed trials where the fastest dog completing every obstacle wins. In Australia's "three sheep" trial, the handler walks with the dog, and its "yard" trial tests working chutes and pens. There's a "South Wales" variant (more on that later). But the national trial is the gold standard in the UK, North America, New Zealand, South Africa, and Europe.

At a national trial, the dog runs out to the sheep and comes around behind them without upsetting them (OUTRUN: 20 points). The moment of dog/sheep first acquaintance is the LIFT (10 points). The sheep come off quietly and straight for the FETCH (20 points) through panels to the handler's feet. Proper outwork (outrun, lift, and fetch) is vital and worth 50 of the trial's 100 points.

When the handler goes to the post, he has 100 points. The judge deducts points for every fault; he cannot award them. Any command on the outrun will cost 1 or 2 points, 3 points subtracted for each fetch bobble, 4 or 5 points for missing the fetch gate, and so on.

The outrun, lift, and fetch are the easy points — you can't lose more than 5 or 6 outwork points and hope to be in the money at most national trials. Outwork is vital because it is how the dog introduces himself to the sheep: "Hi there, ladies, I'm Shep. Sorry about disturbing you, but we have

LUKE OUTRUNNING

our work to do." As opposed to: "Sheep, make my day!" or, "Gee, I'm so happy to meet you sheep. I'm not feeling too well at the moment. Mightn't you move?"

If the dog makes a poor first impression, the sheep react badly and the run gets too exciting. If the outwork is good, the sheep arrive calmly at the handler's feet.

Sometimes the sheep fear the crowd behind the handler and won't round the handler's post. The handler can move a crook's length from the post to give them room.

The DRIVE is worth 30 points. Border Collies instinctively gather and fetch sheep; they must be trained to drive them away. If the handler were to quit commanding and fall silent on the drive, the dog would fetch the sheep back to the handler's feet.

At a national trial, the dog drives the sheep away 200 yards or so through the drive panels, then across the course 400 yards or so through the cross-drive panels.

Fetch, drive, and crossdrive panels are freestanding wood or plastic with a 21-foot gap. That sounds like plenty but 400 yards away, 21 feet looks like the eye of a needle.

After missing the crossdrive panels at six consecutive trials I went to an optometrist and was bitterly disappointed when he said there wasn't a damn thing wrong with my eyes.

After the sheep have passed through or missed the drive and/or cross-drive panels, the dog turns them tightly; ideally they will brush the back of the panels.

From thence the sheep are brought into the shedding ring, 40 yards in diameter, marked by close mowing or sawdust clumps because sheep might balk at an unbroken line. After his sheep are in the ring, the handler may join them. Once in the ring, the sheep cannot leave it without deductions.

The handler and dog establish a steady pace and keep the sheep at a brisk walk. When sheep are moving calmly it's easier to keep them on line and through the panels. The slower the sheep walk — without pausing to graze or turn on the dog — the more precise the handler can be. Unfortunately there's a time limit.

There's just enough time so the dog who does good work can finish but the dog who mucks about or has unusual difficulties will be called off with points only for those tasks he's completed. (If he doesn't finish the drive he loses those 30 points plus all the points for later tasks he hasn't attempted.)

As my sheep walk into the shedding ring, I always check my watch hoping I've four minutes for the split, the pen, and the single. If the sheep are hard to shed most of my time will be eaten by the shedding ring, if they're pen-shy at the pen.

Total time? At smaller trials, with 300- or 400-yard outruns, I might have eight or nine minutes. Complex fields with vast outruns might set a twenty-minute limit.

At the SPLIT (10 points) the handler and/or dog creates a space — six, eight, ten inches? — between sheep 1 and 2 and sheep 3 and 4. The dog comes through the flock, turns on those sheep his handler has indicated, and holds them. If only seconds remain, I'll call the dog through without a gap. Hail Mary full of grace . . .

The PEN is worth 10 points. After splitting them, the dog regathers the sheep while his handler jogs to a 12-by-9-foot freestanding pen. An 8-foot rope is attached to the pen gate and the handler grasps that rope until the sheep are in the pen and the gate is closed, or until he runs out of time.

JUNE SHEDDING

Finally, the handler and dog bring the sheep out of the pen for the SINGLE (10 points), in which dog and man shed off one sheep and hold it. Because the last ewe can see her pals escaping and thus is harder to shed, one sheds the last ewe.

That's all there is to a sheepdog trial. To be in the prize list, handler and dog must accomplish these tasks smoothly and elegantly within the allotted time. Top handler Beverly Lambert told me, "In this country twenty years ago, if you made your panels and finished, you'd win a trial. Fifteen years ago, you had to do it properly. Now you have to finish, do it properly, and take chances."

Good sheep flocks are uniform. Nutritional needs, lambing percentages, even how often you trim their hooves vary from breed to breed. No commercial shepherd wants to manage six hundred individuals. The Gettysburg sheep were not uniform. I spotted several distinct white-face breeds and lots of crossbreds. For sixty days the Finals hosts had fed them up so they'd be sound and energetic. None of the sheep had been worked by dogs before. Each handler-dog team would work four sheep: two ewes and two lambs. They were "panic and bolt" sheep. If your dog came on too hard, one ewe would take off for the woods and her three pals could fend for themselves.

The early runs of the best sheepdogs in North America were a shambles. No handler made his panels and the high score (two judges' combined) was an awful 69. Last year's national champion: DQ. Luke's mother: DQ. Dogs that usually beat me failed to hold their sheep on the course, and the sheep ran two young dogs off. I couldn't eat breakfast. Not a bite.

To my surprise, right-hand outruns had gone worse than the left — dogs found difficulties we handlers hadn't. Very few dogs managed the dogleg fetch: if the dog got his sheep to the dogleg post, the sheep beelined for the rock wall and once sheep and dog were behind the wall, the handler couldn't see his dog.

Luke and I were next to last. At 5:45 it was Gettysburg's mini–rush hour. Traffic was heavy on the road closest to the left outrun, and Luke believed those moving cars were his sheep. I decided to send him left anyway — the field was well fenced and Luke couldn't run out in the road.

Luke and I waited in a blind where I but not Luke could watch the team on the field: Linda Tesdahl and Jace. Linda's a dangerous handler and sheepdoggers stand in line to breed gyps to Jace. But this afternoon, even Jace couldn't control these sheep. Linda got her split but failed to pen. (No single was required today.)

So...

We've thirteen minutes. Luke starts without my command as we're walking to the handler's post. I'm rattled and forget to start my timer.

Luke strikes the road; no sheep just cars. I redirect him with a whistle and he turns towards sheep he can't see, races over the ridge out of sight. Where's Luke? Maybe back to the road, maybe he's crossed the course in the swale (19 points off per judge). There! There he is! He hasn't spotted the sheep so I whistle him out again and he takes my command and comes up nicely behind his sheep and I whistle him down but don't insist. If Luke's going to control these rank sheep he has to do so NOW and he's 470 yards nearer them than I am.

His sheep lift nicely and drop into the gully. I don't breathe until they reappear on line for the dogleg post. My brilliant Luke holds them on the dogleg through the fetch panels. Nice turn around me at the post. I've drawn a ewe and her twin lambs plus a single ewe. The twins will want to stick with Mama, so they'll be problems at the split.

As the sheep near the drive panels they want to veer right — back up the field — so Luke blocks them. But as soon as they're through the panels, they bolt up the field and he has to race all the way around — 300 degrees — to catch and bring them back onto the crossdrive line. Luke brings the sheep back, but he's on the far side of that damned wall and the sheep are on the near side.

Heart in my throat, I recall Luke and he clambers over the wall, but Luke is completely, inexplicably out of gas. He is ignoring my commands. If I attempt those crossdrive panels, I believe Luke'll grip (DQ: score zero), so I don't (and accept beaucoup points off). Luke brings the sheep into the shedding ring.

Luke's the best shedding dog I've ever owned and we have time — without a watch I'd guess four minutes — but the judges want that two/two split and Mama's lambs ain't gonna leave Mama's side so Luke and I try and try until time is called. Luke heads for the water tub to roll and splash like a weary porpoise. It's over.

What the hell happened to Luke? He's never quit on me before.

Our score? 69. I expect it'll take 120 to get through to the semifinals.

MY NIECE, Rachael Ashley-Layton, was on our Gettysburg team. She's spent summer vacations on the farm since she was a toddler. Like her father, Rachael is an avid sports fan, and in their LA home one television is tuned to Rachael's game and a second to her father's while computers whir, collecting game scores.

I don't know anything about sports and Anne, who grew up in a sports-mad household, dislikes them. We turn our television on after dinner and no daily sports page arrives in our mailbox. So the desperate, sports-deprived Rachael decided sheepdog trialing just might be a sport after all. When she was fourteen, she, Anne, two sheepdogs, and I drove to Kingston, Ontario, for the Grass Creek sheepdog trial. It's my favorite trial, held in a beautiful park on the St. Lawrence River.

Saturdays and Sundays, the trial draws twenty thousand spectators, and by ten o'clock cars are lined up outside waiting for someone to leave so they can get in. At the end of the day, after the spectators are gone, sheepdogs are turned out to romp and chase on the sandy beach. They lift doggy rooster tails through the bright shallows.

At the time I was running old Silk and wee, timid Josie. During the twelve-hour drive from farm to Canada, Rachael coached the dogs: "You can do it! You can win! Quitters never win and winners never quit!" Come the day, as Silk and I waited to go on the course, young Rachael knelt to whisper encouragement in Silk's ear. If Rachael'd been Christian she'd have led Silk in prayer.

Well, Silk lost her sheep and was too old to catch them, and when those tough sheep turned on her, poor scared Josie jumped straight up in the air. Her eyes were popping out of her head and I could almost hear her crying "Help! Help!"

Net score for two dogs? Zero.

I thought it was funny. Rachael was not amused and it was a long, very silent drive back home. Rachael wouldn't speak to me or the dogs for days.

THE NEXT YEAR Rach decided to get in the game. Rules say a sheep-dog like Silk, who has competed in a national trial, can never again run in a novice class. But sheepdoggers aren't rule fanatics, most are parents or grandparents, and here was this LA kid who saw sheep just three weeks a year and wanted to compete in novice with Silk — so what the hey?

Unfortunately, Silk didn't wish to work with Rachael.

At Roy Johnson's novice trial I told Rach, "Unclip Silk from the car, walk straight to the trial field. Don't say one word to Silk before you send her. I'll be hiding where she can't see me and maybe you can fool her. Good luck."

In the quarter-acre novice field, Silk's professional skills kicked in and she made a perfect outrun, lift, and fetch, but as she approached Rachael, Silk had an epiphany —"MY HANDLER IS NOT DONALD"— and she quit working. Since a dog is disqualified if it leaves the field, mamas and grandmamas blocked the gate so Silk couldn't escape and Roy's sheep were so dog-broke they followed Rach *without a dog behind them.* Sans Silk, Rach couldn't pen, but she won the "Most Promising Handler" badge to take back with her to LA.

Rachael and June were love at first sight. During Rachael's precious time on the farm June slept on Rachael's bed and only the Angeleno Kid worked my gyp.

One fine Saturday, Ms. Rachael Ashley-Layton and June won a novice trial, and I pretended I didn't see my niece behind the handler's tent, hugging June and weeping.

Which is how Rachael became June's life coach. Or maybe the other way round. Anyway, Rachael skipped orientation at the University of Texas to fly to Gettysburg and coach June through the National Finals.

Our motel was a grungy pine-paneled relic of the fifties. In five days I never saw a housekeeper, and Rachael wouldn't shower because she didn't trust her toes to the mold. The motel did have a big field where the dogs could run. Dogs don't fear grunge.

June ran Friday in the late afternoon, the hottest part of the day, which usually makes sheep cranky. After being penned up all day, they'd be hungry and hard to move. When we went to the post June really wanted to go left (she'd spotted those rush-hour cars), but she's a shallower outrunner than Luke, and although she'd take my redirect I worried that once she got over that first ridge she'd drop into the swale and reappear (as many had before) crossed over to the wrong side of the course (19 points off per judge).

The sheepdog's outrun is supposed to be genetic so every command until the dog gets behind the sheep is points off. I set June up on the right, punched my watch, and sent her. As expected, she promptly veered left. I whistled "down" and "away to me." She took my redirect but veered left again. Voice: "Down"; whistled: "Away." This third time, June finally got it and she sailed around the stone wall and the rest of her outrun was just fine. Her lift was fine too: the sheep came off quietly. After disappearing into the swale, they reappeared at the dogleg post. June was invisible, tucked in behind her sheep, so my commands were prompted by what the sheep were doing. They wanted to slip downhill to get behind the stone wall which meant Trouble so I asked June to keep them higher than they preferred. They were slightly off line to the fetch panels but went through. Two ewes, two lambs, and as they approached the handler's post, I breathed easier: none of this miniflock were related. There'd be no mother-and-child reunions in this shedding ring.

As they turned the post, the sheep noticed the shade under the tents and thought to go there, but June forestalled them. The sheep didn't wanna walk back into the blazing sun but June persuaded them. Onto the drive panels: MISTAKE! As the crowd groaned the sheep slipped across the FRONT of the panels. EXPENSIVE mistake.

Crossdrive panels are hard to hit. Often you can't tell where the sheep are in relation to the opening until they're in it, or have missed high or low. At Gettysburg, that rock wall rose uphill behind the crossdrive line. The handler could guesstimate whether his sheep were on line by the sheep's relationship to the wall beside them: if they seemed to be growing taller as they trudged toward the panels, they were on line.

I kept June well back as the sheep walked forward, getting taller and taller. At the last instant I downed June and the sheep drifted through. Bullseye!

June turned and brought her sheep into the shedding ring. I couldn't leave the post until the first sheep put her hoof into the ring but with only two minutes left my body was aching.

In! I ran to block my miniflock, called June around, threatened the sheep, and the two ewes bolted giving me my opening. I called June in and she turned the two lambs. "Good!" the judge shouted.

Fifty-one seconds left as I jogged to the pen. I called June around as I jerked the gate open and snatched up the rope. Gate/rope/Donald/Donald's crook blocked the sheep on one side. June blocked the other.

Thirty seconds left. SECOND MISTAKE: I pressed too hard. Three sheep went in the pen but one ewe slipped past and the others came out and the course director called "Thank you" before I could try again.

"Thank you" means "You're disqualified: score zero." What'd I do? Huh? As I bent to pat June, the pickup dog collected her sheep and a lamb jumped over the pickup dog to the spectators' laughter and applause.

The course director, a courtly gent in a white straw cowboy hat, met me at the gate to explain that I hadn't been DQed, he'd meant to call "Time." I thanked him.

June found shade and a tub of cold water. Handlers came over to congratulate us.

Tommy Wilson, June's breeder, said, "She went well."

"She's well-bred."

Tommy laughed.

I added, "I rushed the pen."

"Aye. Easy to do."

Rachael grinned. "June's in the semifinals. She's got to be in!"

I shrugged.

I couldn't bear waiting for our score so I handed June to Rachael and started to the car. I'd walk Luke and sort myself out.

My friend Pearse Ward intercepted me. "I think you just knocked me out," he said. Pearse was "on the bubble": lowest scoring handler in the top forty.

"I dunno. How many points do you have?"

"Hundred eighteen."

Rachael ran to us, laughing and shaking her head. "One twenty-seven. June's in!"

Behaviorism

Skinner's conception of science is very odd.
— Noam Chomsky

TRADITIONAL DOG training is anecdotal. Bill Koehler believed dog behavior was profoundly ethical, and Vicki Hearne elaborated on Koehler's theory, but most traditional trainers are simple pragmatists, and success with a difficult dog trumps epistemology every time. To date, e-collar trainers are pretheoretical: no thinker has explained how the new variable-intensity e-collar helps a dog learn.

The traditional pet training curriculum wasn't formalized until the eve of World War II, and expanded in postwar suburbs where veterans wanted a wife, a house, two children, a Chevy, and a family dog — preferably a purebred dog. Most prominent dog trainers, like Koehler, got their experience training war dogs — big, powerful "manstoppers" — and except for women competing in AKC obedience trials, most trainers were men.

Two years after the AKC started its obedience trials, eight years before Blanche Saunders published her first training book, and eighteen years before Bill Koehler published his, B. F. Skinner's *The Behavior of Organisms* was rocking psychology departments.

Skinner didn't find "behaviorism" under a cabbage leaf. Its reductionist, skeptical epistemology (theory of knowledge) was British empiricism taken to its radical extreme.

I studied philosophy at Montana State University with Dr. Cynthia Schuster, a tall, brilliant empiricist who'd studied with Rudolf Carnap and Hans Reichenbach, logical positivists who insisted that what wasn't observable and quantifiable was illusory. Positivists dismissed the philosophers' "substance" as well as the theologians' "soul" and "God" and consigned "ethics," "metaphysics," "emotions," and "instinctual" behaviors to the intellectual rubbish heap.

No, they were not kidding: When Hans Reichenbach published an article denying ethics were knowledge, a colleague stormed into his seminar. "Hans, you cannot mean this! Look. In 1933 when Hitler dismissed you from the University of Berlin, you knew that he was wrong and you knew that you were right. So how can you pretend this stuff about no knowledge in ethics?"

Reichenbach replied, "What you do not understand is that I do believe what I have said. I did not like Hitler's aims. He did not like mine. He had power. Fortunately I was able to get out and come to a place where people's desires and aims were more like mine. But I do not see how I could claim to know that Hitler was wrong and I was right. Such claims to knowledge do not stand up to the criteria by which I define knowledge."

In the 1890s, Ivan Pavlov removed dogs' salivary glands to quantify their saliva production and proved scientifically that dogs salivated not only when food appeared but at a ringing bell associated with previous meals. For this cruel proof of what any beginning dog trainer could have told him, Pavlov won the Nobel Prize.

John Watson popularized Pavlov's theories in the US:

Psychology as the behaviorist views it is a purely objective experimental branch of natural science. Its theoretical goal is the prediction and control of behavior. Introspection forms no essential part of its methods, nor is the scientific value of its data dependent upon the readiness with which they lend themselves to interpretation in terms of consciousness. The behaviorist, in his efforts to get a unitary scheme of animal response, recognizes no dividing line between man and brute.

Nineteenth-century psychology was the philosophy of mind — think William James. The behaviorists had "physics envy," abjuring those fuzzy philosophical theories and aspiring to be a hard science. They quit publishing in philosophical journals and founded their own damn journals. Watson's refusal to recognize a dividing line between man and animal sparked a bonanza of animal experimentation that would, behaviorists believed, produce a verifiable science of human behavior.

They were anti-Darwinians. In the nature/nurture debate behaviorists came down foursquare for nurture: all behaviors were created and all behaviors were equal. Complex behaviors could be shaped from simpler ones, properly reinforced.

Exporting their theories of learning to human subjects didn't work well. Watson's film of Little Albert, a "fear conditioned" eleven-month-old infant, was more distressing than convincing, and subsequent attempts by Watson to demonstrate human conditioning persuaded no one.

Watson's theories were becoming curiosa when B. F. Skinner revivified and radicalized them.

B. F. Skinner was a cultivated, original thinker, canny inventor, and world-class crackpot. His *The Behavior of Organisms* was and is the behaviorist bible. He invented the Skinner box: a closed environment where the effects of unique stimuli on rat, pigeon, and small primate learning could be measured by instruments. Many who've never seen a Skinner box have a fair idea how they work. The rat pulls a lever and gets a reward. Right?

More or less. The experimenter (likely some bored grad student) doesn't need to watch the rat, he just changes the instrument's batteries.

For the rat, the Skinner box is a slot machine he's locked inside.

LIKE POSITIVISM, its philosophical cousin, behaviorism offered a reductionist view of experience, which would clear away foggy old misconceptions like freedom and dignity and usher in true human happiness.

Skinner believed there were four and only four ways mammalian behavior can be changed:

1. Positive reinforcement: Following a behavior with something the animal perceives as pleasant will increase the behavior. (Give the dog a treat after it does as bid and the dog will — over time — do it more frequently.)

2. Negative punishment: Following a behavior with removing something the animal perceives as pleasant will decrease the behavior. (If you don't greet the dog that jumps up on you, the absence of expected affection will — over time — decrease the jumping up.)

3. Positive punishment: Following a behavior with something the dog perceives as unpleasant will decrease the behavior. (If you knee the dog that jumps on you, he'll quit doing it.)

4. Negative reinforcement: Following a behavior by removing something the animal perceives as unpleasant will increase the behavior. (If you stop shocking the dog he'll do what you want.)

In 1962, most psychologists were Skinnerites, and to pass Psych 101 at Montana State University, we undergraduates spent many dismal hours doing their experiments. (Remember the "rotary pursuit"?)

"Behavior modification" was the behaviorists' explicit goal. After their experiments produced enough verifiable, quantifiable knowledge, dispassionate Doctors of Psychology (who better?) would modify educational and penal policies to inform the young, reform the wicked, and cure the mad. A fair number of insane asylums and schools for the retarded eagerly adopted Skinner's learning model. Skinner claimed particular success with autistic children.

Five years after I left MSU, my son, Jon, was diagnosed as autistic and profoundly retarded. Jon's training school used behavior modification. "It's important," they assured me, "that he learn simple behaviors": how to eat with a fork, how to brush his own teeth. "Even if Jon must spend his life institutionalized, he can learn to brush his own teeth."

Behavior modification for humans did not survive legal challenges by civil rights groups, who argued not that the methods were necessarily cruel (although undoubtedly some were), but that there was no evidence the methods worked.

When Jon was twenty-five all his rotted teeth were extracted so it probably doesn't matter that he never learned to brush them.

NO MATTER HOW MANY Skinner boxes they constructed nor how many students were dragooned into experiments, the prestige of hard science eluded the behaviorists.

European psychologists like Piaget developed competitive learning theories but the most important dissent came from within behaviorist ranks. In 1959 researcher Harry Harlow designed an experiment in which eight baby monkeys were placed in cages equipped with wire and cloth monkey "mothers." The wire mothers dispensed milk, the cloth mothers did not. Alas for theory: the baby monkeys clung to the cloth monkeys and only went to the wire monkeys to eat. There's a famous photograph of a monkey clinging to the cloth mother with his hind legs while leaning to the wire mother for a snack.

Two years later, Skinner disciples Keller and Marian Breland described more disappointments:

> When we began this work, it was our aim to see if the science would work beyond the laboratory, to determine if animal psychology could stand on its own feet as an engineering discipline. These aims have been realized. We have controlled a wide range of animal behavior and have made use of the great popular appeal of animals to make it an economically feasible project.... Thirty-eight species, totaling over 6,000 individual animals, have been conditioned, and we have dared to tackle such unlikely subjects as reindeer, cockatoos, raccoons, porpoises, and whales.
>
> Emboldened by this consistent reinforcement, we have ventured further and further from the security of the Skinner box. However, in this cavalier extrapolation, we have run afoul of a persistent pattern of discomforting failures. These failures, although disconcertingly frequent and seemingly diverse, fall into a very interesting pattern. They all represent breakdowns of conditioned operant behavior.

In one instance,

> a pig was conditioned to pick up large wooden coins and deposit them in a large "piggy bank." The coins were placed several feet from the bank and the pig required to carry them to the bank and deposit them, usually four or five coins for one reinforcement....
>
> ...At first the pig would eagerly pick up one dollar, carry it to the bank, run back, get another, carry it rapidly and neatly, and so on, until the ratio was complete. Thereafter, over a period of weeks the behavior would become slower and slower. He might run over eagerly for each dollar, but on the way back, instead of carrying the dollar and depositing it simply and cleanly, he would repeatedly drop it, root it, drop it again, root it along the way, pick it up, toss it up in the air, drop it, root it some more, and so on.
>
> We thought this behavior might simply be the dilly-dallying of an animal on a low drive. However, the behavior persisted and gained in strength in spite of a severely increased drive — he finally went through the ratios so slowly that he did not get enough to eat in the course of a day. Finally

it would take the pig about 10 minutes to transport four coins a distance of about 6 feet. This problem behavior developed repeatedly in successive pigs. . . .

These egregious failures came as a rather considerable shock to us, for there was nothing in our background in behaviorism to prepare us for such gross inabilities to predict and control the behavior of animals with which we had been working for years. . . .

. . . The diagnosis of theory failure does not depend on subtle statistical interpretations or on semantic legerdemain — the animal simply does not do what he has been conditioned to do.

The Brelands called their study "The Misbehavior of Organisms."

IN *Control: A History of Behavioral Psychology,* Dr. John Mills wrote:

Skinner's values were a set of pretheoretical assumptions that were incorporated into unstated axioms from which the principles guiding his theory and his research practices were derived. The axioms were, first, a commitment to positivism (the data language had to be concrete and had to refer only to observable events) and, second, the belief that animals and humans were guided by a very narrow form of individualistic utilitarianism. Skinner believed, in effect, that an organism would perform an act if and only if it brought immediate gain. Effectively, Skinnerians place laboratory animals under constraints that satisfy those principles. They then conclude that their data and their laws of behavior fully explain all human behavior with no exceptions whatsoever.

SKINNER STOPPED experimenting. He tried to interest the Air Force in "smart bombs" guided by trained pigeons. He invented and marketed the "air-crib," a waist-high, glass-fronted humidity- and temperature-controlled box (aka the "Baby Tender"). He wrote until — literally — the day before he died.

Skinner box instruments let grad students measure animal behaviors without watching the animals. So they didn't.

Behaviorism has fallen out of favor with academic psychologists skeptical of its methodology, its sweeping claims, and its usefulness. When a theory is designed to control humans and beasts and fails to do so, the theory joins phrenology in the cabinet of unscientific curiosa.

But never mind! In 1984, with a blurb from Skinner himself, behaviorism came roaring back with Karen Pryor's book *Don't Shoot the Dog*, which promised:

> This book is about how to train anyone — human or animal, young or old, oneself or others — to do anything that can and should be done. How to get the cat off the kitchen table or your grandmother to stop nagging you. How to affect behavior in your pets, your kids, your boss, your friends. How to improve your tennis stroke, your golf game, your math skills, your memory. All by using the principles of training with reinforcement.
>
> These principles are laws, like the laws of physics. They underlie all learning-teaching situations as surely as the law of gravity underlies the falling of an apple. Whenever we attempt to change behavior, in ourselves or in others, we are using these laws, whether we know it or not.

Karen Pryor adapted behaviorism to dog training and helped found the "purely positive" training movement.

Ms. Pryor has a BA from Cornell and trained dolphins at Hawaii's Sea Life Park and Oceanic Institute before she brought Skinner's theories — and a gadget called a clicker — to dog training. Pryor's brilliant, compelling analogy might be paraphrased: "If I can train wild dolphins and orcas to do tricks with food rewards and clicker conditioning, why won't the same principles work for pet dogs (and humans)?"

The analogy is appealing. One envisions tremendous sea creatures, previously wild predators, leaping happily out of the water, performing elaborate tricks to kids' delighted giggles and their elders' astonishment and applause. Why wouldn't such training work with the family dog?

On the other hand, the dolphin pool is nothing more nor less than an aquatic Skinner box, with the Skinner box's advantages (absolute control of every element) and its disadvantages too.

Heather Houlahan criticizes the first half of the analogy:

Okay, first, I would hire men with powerboats and harpoons and nets to terrorize and kidnap the whale — a powerful wild predator with complex social relations and strong family connections — pull him out of the water, rendering him completely helpless, and take him away from his family and his home range of many hundreds of square miles.

Then I would put him in a tiny shallow sensory deprivation tank, full of stinking chlorinated water, where his sonar signals and all his distress vocalizations bounce off concrete walls and come back to blast him.

Then I'd deprive him of his natural food and opportunities to hunt and eat normally, and force him to eat the frozen chum that I provide, by hand. (Has the Geneva Convention kicked in yet?) After enough time he might be Keikoized — incapable of catching his own prey, and so completely dependent on hand-delivered chum.

Then I'd make all access to that chum contingent on him performing the "behaviors" that I require of him. No trick, no eat. . . .

Want to know the rest, or has that been "gentle," "positive," and "kindly" enough for you?

The American Veterinary Society of Animal Behavior takes Pryor's part:

Choosing a dog trainer can be one of the most important decisions that you make in your dog's life. . . . AVSAB endorses training methods which allow animals to work for things (e.g., food, play, affection) that motivate them rather than techniques that focus on using fear or pain to punish them for undesirable behaviors. . . .

Therefore, trainers who routinely use choke collars, pinch collars, shock collars, and other methods of physical punishment as a primary training method should be avoided.

I'D GUESS THAT today, behaviorist/"positive" trainers outnumber Koehler, e-collar, and drive trainers combined. Their professional organization, the Association of Pet Dog Trainers (APDT), boasts four times as many members as the IACP, its traditional competitor. Bo, President Obama's dog, was trained by a positive trainer. Traditional trainers argue that positive training is slow, unreliable, and substitutes "management" for training. They claim no champion obedience trial dog has ever been exclusively trained with positive methods; but most agility and flyball dogs are so trained. Nobody doubts tricks are easier to teach with positive methods, and in his *Dog Tricks,* Captain Haggerty, a prominent traditional trainer, recommends treat motivators.

Some positive trainers concede their methods take longer and require more "management" than traditional training, but, they add, their methods are less likely to cause problems than over-harsh or ill-applied punishments. Positive training, they claim, encourages the dog to offer more behaviors.

Positive trainers claim theirs is the only scientifically proven training method, and whatever one thinks of their "science" claim, behaviorism is a systematic learning theory.

Time-challenged pet owners uncomfortable with traditional trainers' anecdotes may find consistent, easier to understand answers in Dr. Skinner's theories.

And, if one must choose between "Positive Training" and — what is the alternative anyway? Negative training? Cruel training? — that's a no-brainer.

Positive Trainer Pat Miller

The question, then, is this: Would you rather hurt your dog
to train him — or feed him treats? Seems obvious, doesn't it?
— Pat Miller

A CERTIFICATE FROM the Association of Pet Dog Trainers states
that Pat Miller is a certified pet dog trainer, and another from
the American Veterinary Society of Animal Behavior says she
is a certified dog behavioral consultant. Beside the certificates in Miller's
training room is a photograph taken when Miller was a uniformed animal
control officer for the Marin County, California, SPCA. The young woman
in the photo is sternly beautiful, and some years later Miller is an unusually
handsome woman.

The animal welfare connection continues. Pat's husband, Paul, heads
the county SPCA, and my first visit was abbreviated because the Millers
had just rescued seventy starving horses from an animal hoarder and were
caring for them at a nearby farm and on Peaceable Paws, their eighty-acre
Maryland spread.

Their farm is a pretty place; the entry lane is bordered by woods and a
meadow where dog agility equipment is scattered about.

Pat Miller has authored (among other books) *The Power of Positive
Dog Training* (2001), *Positive Perspectives: Love Your Dog, Train Your Dog*
(2004), and *Positive Perspectives 2: Know Your Dog, Train Your Dog* (2008),
as well as pamphlets, articles, and reviews in *Whole Dog Journal* and *Bark*
magazine. She is past president of the Association of Pet Dog Trainers.

Once she was a traditional trainer, whose terrier mix, Josie, had earned
her Companion Dog and Companion Dog Excellent titles from the AKC.
But Josie couldn't complete the retrieving requirement for the next rung
in competitive obedience, Utility Dog. Miller's fellow trainers urged her to
use the ear pinch (a Koehler technique) to improve Josie's retrieving, and

Pat pinched faithfully "until one afternoon when I got out the training equipment and Josie, who had always been a willing and happy worker, hid under the deck and refused to come out."

Distressed at Josie's reaction, Miller quit training for months, until one day she heard about "Positive Training," which used treats and a clicker/marker instead of corrections. Josie never got her UD but she had a long and happy life. These days, Miller doesn't compete her dogs. She owns seven, all rescues.

As she and I talked, Luke and June sat blissfully at Pat's feet. She never stopped stroking them.

I visited the second week of Pat's adult dog class. (No dogs are present the first week when behaviorist methods and philosophy are explained.) Since it's hard to persuade owners to stick with a lengthy training program, Miller finesses the problem by training for "levels" that the dog and owner can attain without reference to how many weeks it takes.

Level 1 skills are:

1. *Name response*
   Dog responds promptly to her name at least 8 of 10 times. Owner demonstrates understanding of not repeating name if dog doesn't respond, but uses (kissy noise) or some other sound to get response.

2. *Stationary attention*
   Owner can keep dog's attention for 5 seconds with mild distractions.

3. *Sits*
   Dog sits on verbal cue at least 8 of 10 times (prompting allowed).

4. *Greetings*
   Dog sits for greetings at least 8 of 10 times and does not jump up.

5. *Handling*
   Owner and instructors can handle dog's ears and paws.

6. *Owner skill*
   Can recognize and fix tight leash.

7. *Owner skill*
   Understands concept of reward marking and has reasonably good mechanical skills (timing/click then treat).

Level 4 dogs have achieved the following:

1. *Recalls*

   Comes promptly across room 3 of 3 times, high distractions.

2. *Polite walking*

   Dog walks by owner's side 3 full laps of training area with low rate of reinforcement, moderate distractions.

3. *Leave it*

   Owner can give "Leave it" cue and drop forbidden object without having to body block, 3 of 3 times.

4. *Give*

   Dog will drop moderately high value object on cue without prompting, 4 of 5 times.

5. *Target to hand*

   Dog will move to target hand and touch 4 of 5 times.

6. *Hand signal down*

   Dog will lie down in response to hand signal only, 4 of 5 times.

7. *Distance down*

   Dog will lie down on cue at a distance of 15 feet, 4 of 5 times.

8. *Shaping — go to place*

   Dog will go to his mat on verbal cue 4 of 5 times; taught by shaping.

9. *Trick*

   Shake, high five, wave, relax, possum, roll over. . . .

10. *Owner skill*

    Understands the concept of shaping and can use to teach a behavior.

Miller's beginning classes are taught by her assistant, Shirley Greenlief, who became a dog trainer a year ago after studying with Pat. Two in-training apprentices assist Shirley. The class has a trainer for every three dogs.

At one end of the training room, portable plastic barriers segregate aggressive (reactive) or timid dogs. The tethers lining the walls are short, plastic-covered cables attached to eyebolts some eighteen inches above the floor. While Miller opposes keeping dogs chained for confinement, she argues strongly for tethering during early training and for home management in the owner's presence. Like the Skinner box or the tank at Sea-World, tether-training maximizes human control.

No trainer is 100 percent management or 100 percent training. The night after I butcher a deer (surrounded by extremely friendly sheepdogs), I crate those dogs most likely to react to diet change by pooping on the floor. Crated, they must restrain themselves or whine me awake to let them outdoors.

When visitors drive down our lane and noisy kids pile out of the car, I *could* let the dogs out to greet them and, if I kept a sharp eye on six sheepdogs and three big sheep-guarding dogs, correcting each dog by name, probably nothing untoward would happen. Probably. But visitors to our remote farm are rare; excited, dashing children invite doggy pursuit; and my dogs can get from zero to sixty in no time.

In pack delirium the dogs are more likely to jump up on visitors or nip children's heels or settle grudges amongst themselves. Since I desire none of these, while my visitors are puzzling over why their host isn't greeting them, I'm busy crating sheepdogs.

At Thanksgiving we feed eighteen people; all ages, in good and poor health. After the first course those who wish to do so join me, Anne, and the dogs on our ritual dog walk. When we come back into the house I crate every dog except June because I can't pay attention to them. But by the end of the evening, as we humans are relaxing by the fire, six sheepdogs will be sprawling about, too.

THERE WERE NO aggressive dogs in Ms. Greenlief's class, just one timid Peekapoo somewhere behind the barriers. He's been "Abused," I was told. Everything was hyper-cheerful: chirps punctuated by clickers, "Good doggy!," and small treats produced nonstop. Some dogs were puzzled, some were anxious, some barked. When one Corgi's owner clamped her barking dog's mouth shut, an apprentice swiftly provided a peanut butter–stuffed bone to keep the dog's mouth occupied.

Owners were shown how to lure their dogs into a down. "You're training the dog or the dog is training you," Ms. Greenlief advised. "Remember, click then treat, click then treat."

June snoozed behind my chair. I wondered what the student dogs made of the chirping, the constraints, and the intense humans in their faces.

FIVE WEEKS LATER I returned for class graduation. Tethered dogs more or less sat and laid down for treats. As before, they barked. Although I was told that the timid Peekapoo was less timid than she'd been, I couldn't see it. Ms. Greenlief awarded treats to dogs whose owners were in their turn awarded cardboard bones for improved dog behavior. These could be exchanged for doggy items: toys, treat bags, travel cups, etc.

I thought those cardboard bones rather too deferential to behaviorist theory — wouldn't a mannerly dog be reward enough?

After class, some of the best behaved, less timid dogs were allowed five minutes of untethered freedom running up and down the room. June opened one eye and yawned.

I HAD SEEN Pat Miller's methods applied but I wanted to see Miller herself working a dog. She invited me to an advanced training class called "My Dog Can Do That."

I sat with June in Miller's office browsing *Canine Body Language,* Brenda Aloff's splendid photo collection of dogs' body "utterances."

June stood to greet Ms. Greenlief, who was late for a training appointment with a "dog-reactive" dog. Worried June would barge past her into the training room (with the "dog-reactive" dog), Ms. Greenlief asked June, "Do you know 'wait'?"

I was more puzzled by that question than June was. June is pretty relaxed about human babble. I often feed my dogs in crates and since I don't want them upsetting their food bowls when they come out, I tell them to wait until I've removed the bowls. June knows that when I say "Wait!" she should pause. Provided, of course, that I mean "Wait" instead of "Will you please wait?" or "If you loved me, you'd wait" or "I'm panicking and instead of aggravating my panic, you wait!" or "I'm absolutely furious so you better goddamned wait!!!"

And I'd better say "Wait!" exactly as June is used to hearing it; no slurred speech, no fevered delirium.

And it better be Donald saying "Wait," not some stranger. Dog commands are contextual. I start a sheepdog on voice commands, but as the dog perfects his skills I introduce whistle commands. Whistles are less emotional, more precise, and can be heard for miles in calm weather. Some trainers have unique whistles for each of their dogs. But my dogs are on identical whistles: a sharp descending F above high C to D means "Lie down."

When I ran Luke and June in the Caledonia, Wisconsin, trial, I was midway through a tooth implant: defective tooth extracted, self-tapping dental screw screwed in, but no new tooth as yet. Seven hundred and thirty-five yards from my feet, June couldn't understand any of my whistles. They sounded samey/same to me, but to June my toothless whistles might as well have been Chinese.

When I'm training a young dog, June's my backup. If the trainee dog freaks and scatters sheep to all corners of the known universe, June restores order. Sometimes June must down-stay for ten or twenty minutes while I work the young dog all around her, and though I'm working the young dog on June's whistles June must not budge.

What did Ms. Greenlief's "Do you know 'wait'" mean to June? June knit her brows.

Many pet dog trainers believe one utters dog commands like a drill sergeant. "Heel!" means "Heel!" means "Heel!" The utterer's personal authority, the actual sound he/she makes, and the context shouldn't matter. "Heel" means "Heel" if Armageddon is brightening the skies.

Phooey.

"June," I said, "get over here," and Ms. Greenlief went in to train her "dog-reactive" dog while I mulled over the nuances of how we talk to our dogs.

MY DOG CAN DO THAT! is a board game invented by trainers Dr. Ian Dunbar and Terry Ryan. To advance around the board, competitors draw dog-trick cards from the deck and must train that trick within thirty seconds.

Using the cards without the board, a dozen dogs can compete, and Pat Miller has hosted several My Dog Can Do That! tournaments.

Pat adopted her Corgi, Lucy, three and half years ago. Pat's client told me she'd adopted Star, a Border Collie, from a "working home."

Star detested me. From time to time — i.e., whenever she came near — Star would charge to the end of her leash, barking hysterically. I thought Star was bluffing and 'twere it my class I would have told Star's owner to drop the leash and we'd see what Star would do. But it wasn't my class nor my place to say anything.

Star's owner had competed in AKC obedience trials until she was introduced to Pat's methods. "They're so much better!" she gushed. "I do rally now." (Rally is simplified obedience.)

Lured with treats, Lucy and Star did figure-eights through their trainers' legs. They sat and shook their heads from side to side (card: "Sitting up and saluting"). They lay down, legs fully extended, for ten seconds. They shook their heads vigorously up and down and from side to side ("I'm losing my mind").

Whenever Star remembered I was there she'd lunge, yapping. I sat quietly, didn't speak, and kept my gaze off her. The dogs did the "around and through" exercise and "catch three treats in a row."

"Drop them in," Pat Miller advised, "until Star gets the idea." From time to time, Star charged me. When Star's owner mused, "Funny thing. My first Border Collie didn't like men either," I couldn't resist, "What do you think about men?"

"They're all right, I guess."

Pat Miller and Lucy made a fine team. Miller's graceful moves complemented her dog's happy attentiveness.

The dog trainer's expectations, communicated lucidly and consistently, trump methodology, and despite very different methods, Pat Miller, Tony Ancheta, and Behesha Doan are brilliant, lucid trainers. After the training session ended and Star left, June wandered over to notify Lucy that June was the top gyp on premises. Lucy didn't have a problem with that.

One of the quiet pleasures of working dogs is listening in on doggy conversations. For June and Lucy, the humans were peripheral to their meet and greet, but Pat and I could hear everything they said.

The Last Dog Still Standing

I'D RUN IN FIVE National Finals but reached the semifinals only once and never gotten through to the finals — the top 17 dogs. At the 1994 Finals in Lexington, Kentucky, I'd been out by only 2 points.

More handlers are winnowed in the qualifying round — 110 of 150 — than during the semifinals: 23 out, 17 in. Though the better handlers and dogs get most of the luck there's a little left for me and June, and I had almost a 50/50 chance of getting into the Finals, which would certainly qualify us for the United States Team.

That's all June and I needed to do — defeat 23 dog/handler teams that usually creamed us. Hell, where's my passport? Might as well start packing my bag!

June won $200 by reaching this plateau: $15 more than her entry fee. Stick with me, honey, and I'll turn your money green!

That night I lay on my lumpy motel bed, rerunning June's run in my head; too tired to think, too excited to sleep.

June slept in Rachael's room. June needed Rachael's snuggle for her big day tomorrow.

GETTYSBURG ENJOYED a bright, clear Saturday. Behind the big, empty trial field sprawled a gypsy encampment of billowing tents and vendor vans. Across the road, RVs, trailers, and backpacking tents filled the handlers' campground. Handlers and dogs traveling by golf carts, ATVs, and shank's mare whisked across the road while rent-a-cops halted traffic. The Finals paid the cops, setout crew, and judges. The other workers were volunteers. The scorekeepers, runners, judges' minders, course director, gate and parking attendants, those who arranged the flowers in the handlers' tent and served the complimentary cold drinks, fruit, and pastries: nobody got a dime. Some volunteers drove a thousand miles at their own expense for the privilege of working here.

Vendors sold sausages, burgers, hot dogs — pretty much what you'd expect — and Boy Scout mothers peddled baked goods. You could buy weaving/spinning/knitting products and anything your dog might want.

Last night, the Harley dealer sponsored a dinner dance in his showroom, and that's what the handlers were reliving as they drank coffee and sucked donut sugar from their fingers. They talked about dancing and, of course, dogs.

"I don't know if Shep will face down these sheep; if they turn on him ..."

"Hell, I haven't had my dogs out much this summer ..."

So forth and so on ...

By custom, most sheepdog trials welcome mannerly noncompeting pets. Most dogs under the handlers' tent were sheepdogs but there were a miniature Dachshund, a few Terriers, and some mutts, too. Heather Houlahan brought a young, nervy English Shepherd to socialize among the mannerly dogs and dog-savvy people. In three decades, I have never seen a dogfight at a sheepdog trial.

Despite her husband Scott's vocal opposition to "useless pets," Jenny Glenn had an exuberant, ratty mutt at her feet. Seems Scott and Jenny were driving across the Dakotas, clipping along pretty fast behind a kid driving a pickup whose little dog was bouncing around in the bed. They were laughing at the dog's antics until it kamikaze-jumped out of the truck. Scott blew a tire swerving to miss him. Once they got stopped, they came back and carried the dog off the road.

They waited on the prairie for the pickup's driver to return for his dog but he didn't. "I guess he was scared," Jenny said.

After a couple hours, the little dog was up and playing with their Border Collies. "Scott swore he'd never get anything but a sheepdog, never ..."

Jenny smiled at her dog. The dog smiled back. "This is 'Skid,'" she said. "It cost seventy dollars to replace that darn tire."

The trial committee had eliminated the dogleg fetch and instead of a split then pen, dog and handler must split any two, then pen all five and shed a single. Fifteen minutes. Possible two-judge score: 220 points.

June and I drew the thirty-seventh slot and would run late afternoon, same as yesterday. I had hours to kill.

I was scheduled to do a signing for *The Dog Wars,* and a familiar face was waiting at the table. Bob McGowan had been an AKC vice president when we Border Collie people fought against AKC recognition — the fight *The Dog Wars* describes. AKC officials like McGowan may have honestly believed that, without ever breeding, rearing, training, trialing, or working one Border Collie, they knew better than those who'd spent decades with the dog how to shepherd the Border Collie breed. People can believe anything with a little effort.

"You'll like this one better." I urged my essay collection, *A Useful Dog,* on McGowan, but he bought *The Dog Wars* too.

Beverly Lambert's ten-year-old Pippa had come second at last year's Finals. At Gettysburg, Pippa's run was as close to perfect, as utterly beautiful, as it could be. When her score was announced the handlers' tent exploded with cheers: 205 points.

Although I wished it was my dog creating such beauty, I was grateful another's dog could.

It had gotten too hot to leave my dogs in the car so I chained them to the bumper. They had shade and drinking water underneath the car. When I chain dogs thus, I clip my ignition key to the chain so that no matter what, I cannot drive off without unfastening them. I know a vet who got an emergency call and . . .

The breeze died and the handlers' tent was hot and airless. I watched from the shadow of a construction trailer, Francis Raley's temporary HQ.

One of the rent-a-cops delivered June. "Is she yours?"

The clip attaching June's chain to her collar had come undone and June was freed. Loose dog in a big public event is a bad thing. Potentially, a very bad thing. Like the sensible gyp she is, June walked to the rent-a-cops and told them she was lost.

SCORES CRASHED. The sheep last grazed before daylight and by late afternoon they were overheated, hungry, and cranky. Some fought the dog around the course, others bolted to the shady woods.

I checked my watch and whistle and inhaled three zots of albuterol. A spectator asked, "Are you having fun?"

"This is a sheepdog trial. What's fun about that?"

I sat on a hot metal chair in a black plastic blind wondering which of my numerous sins delivered me here. From nose to tail tip, June trembled.

The handler on the field couldn't keep his sheep on the course and re-tired. Oh-boy-our-turn. Wasn't this exactly what I'd been striving for?

In the 1960s, many of us young poets embraced Arthur Rimbaud's prescription for acquiring visions — systematically disorder the senses — never imagining how wobbly the senses are nor how readily they disorder. As I walked toward the handler's post, my sense of smell shut down. I went deaf. I supposed an announcer was introducing me, but couldn't hear a word. At the mouth of my tunnel vision, five hundred yards out, the spot-ter hadn't settled my sheep: they were running this way and that.

I was acutely aware of June, who was prancing sideways, searching my face for last-minute suggestions and her release. June told me that like yes-terday she preferred to outrun left, toward that road. But June ran well on the right yesterday and right it must be. June set up eight feet to my right; she was cocked, curled in an explosive semicircle.

"Away to me."

My whistle was ready in case she needed a redirect, but June executed a flawless outrun and finished behind her sheep. I called her on and though the sheep were heavy they lifted properly and came onto the fetch line and it was a good fetch, through the panels, over the wall — a little off-line here, a point or two deducted — thence to my feet. I'd drawn two big white leaders, two middlings, and a spotty-faced ewe who was having a hard time keeping up with the others. She'd be my single.

Around my feet, a jig and jag at the drive panels but through them, and they turned onto the crossdrive. The sheep were trotting pretty quick and I got in a couple last-second corrections (points off) before three sheep went through the panels. Two missed (more points off).

I had five minutes left and these sheep had been fairly easy to pen and shed. June's wasn't a great run but we were probably in for the Finals. I didn't actually think that thought — didn't have time to think — but maybe the pressure affected my brain because when the ewes came panting into the shedding ring, those two big whitefaces were in the lead and I blocked the last three and called June in and turned her ON THE WRONG DAMN SHEEP. Instantly I realized my mistake and turned June onto the correct sheep who hadn't left the ring. I listened for the judge's "Okay!"

No "Okay"; we must try again.

Whereupon we went to hell in a handbasket.

The sheep were wise to us now. They raced through the ring from one side to the other and I never got them slowed so June could have a second chance. Next time I checked my watch we had one minute left and June's tongue was hanging out and the sheep were stressed and we were toast. So I tipped my hat to the judge and retired June. She beelined for cool water in the tub.

Rachael was painfully disappointed. "Why did you quit?"

Handlers came over to say how much they admired June. Allan Higgenbottom said, "Whatever happened today, yesterday your gyp beat 115 of the best sheepdogs in North America."

Alas, that was yesterday. As June and I trudged toward our car, a respected American judge intercepted us. "They should have called that split," he said.

"I turned her onto the wrong sheep."

"Yes, and that should have been pointed. But she was controlling the proper sheep before they left the ring."

"Well, I wish you'd been sitting in the judge's tent."

"Your gyp had them before they were out of the ring, we all saw it."

Jesus I was tired. "Oh well," I said. "That's sheepdog trialing."

Listening to Dr. Dodman

Think about it. You have removed your pet's need to hunt by supplying food. You have removed his romantic interests by neutering him. You have removed his social need by depriving him of pack interests and competition. He can't even wander and explore his outside territory, let alone try to resolve his own problems — because there aren't any. You saw to that. So what's a poor dog to do? Channel his energies in unacceptable ways, that's what. — Dr. Nicholas Dodman

A RE YOU Max's?" The vet tech smiled at me.
I shook my head no. I didn't think I belonged to any dog, but if I did, I'd probably be Luke's, presently in the car, or June's. She was beside me in the reception room of Tufts University's Foster Hospital for Small Animals.

June eyed the big and little pet dogs and their humans. June yawned. June didn't want Donald to be hers: she had enough on her plate. Besides, how would she feed him?

A slightly embarrassed human confessed he was indeed Max's and followed the tech to the treatment rooms.

I hadn't heard whether I'd made the United States Team. The dogs and I were traveling to a Vermont trial, and I'd detoured to meet Dr. Nicholas Dodman, the man who'd introduced dogs to Prozac.

After the receptionist announced us, June and I strolled to the doctor's office. Tufts is on a beautiful campus with big tree-lined fields any dog would enjoy. When I unclipped June's string leash, she dropped her snout to the grass, investigating a scent-world as intelligible to her as it was mysterious to me.

Dr. Dodman is director of the Tufts Animal Behavior Clinic. His *The Dog Who Loved Too Much: Tales, Treatments, and the Psychology of Dogs*

(1996), *Dogs Behaving Badly: An A-to-Z Guide to Understanding and Curing Behavioral Problems in Dogs* (1999), *Best Behavior: Unleashing Your Dog's Instinct to Obey* (2004), *Puppy's First Steps: The Whole Dog Approach to Raising a Happy, Healthy, Well-Behaved Puppy* (2007), and *The Well-Adjusted Dog: Dr. Dodman's Seven Steps to Lifelong Health and Happiness for Your Best Friend* (2008) have been best-sellers. He has patents for "treatment of repetitive disorders with opioid antagonists" and "treatment of OCD in animals and humans using NMDA blockers." He greeted us affably at the front door of his modest colonial house/office.

When I wrote to request an interview and a chance to watch him work/train his own dog(s), Dr. Dodman replied that he didn't have a dog and, in any case, he was a behavior consultant, not a dog trainer.

Problem for me.

A couple years back, a woman sped down our lane in a cheerful blue minivan. Ours is a working farm and though I am civil to unannounced visitors, I am no more than civil. My visitor was a fan. She asked to let her Border Collies out.

"Sure."

Two dogs ran around and sniffed olfactory messages from the McCaig dog pack. "Well," my fan asked, "what do you think of them?"

I was dumbstruck. I honestly haven't *any* opinion of any sheepdog until I see it work sheep. Anyway, Donald-the-dummkopf answered his fan: "Er, you might want to cut back on their food."

In frosty silence, my visitor jumped her plump dogs back into the van and roared back up the hill.

Another fan done gone. It's not that I have too many.

I don't do theories: I'm a crude American pragmatist. I like hearing dog-training ideas, but absent real live dogs, I can't evaluate them. Scotsman Derek Scrimgeour's training theories are unusual, but Derek has won the Scottish National and anyone can watch his superb dogs work. Scrimgeour's theory is tested by living dogs.

Theories are words. A living dog can or cannot repel an intruder, protect a toddler, have a clean run, be steady to wing and shot, never let up on his tug, or turn a rank old cow. You can or cannot take your pet dog anywhere.

But my interview with Dodman would be dogless. Nicholas Dodman is a clever, amusing writer and talker, but he'd produce no four-footed evidence for his theories. Maybe I could ask June what it all meant.

Dodman introduced me to Ronni, his secretary, before we walked the long, dim hall to his inner sanctum. We'd rescheduled an earlier appointment when he was booked by *Good Morning America* to promote *The Well-Adjusted Dog*. Dodman gave June an absent pat while we gossiped about publishers. He read blurbs for his book from Bo Derek and Jon Stewart.

"June," I asked, "why don't you lie down? Thank you."

Dodman is a charming, hypersmart academic scientist. Like many academics he is fond of his own opinions and a bit unworldly. On second thought, "unworldly" might not be accurate. Unlike yours truly, Dodson was able to get his book on *Good Morning America,* and the client's chair I was sitting in was four inches lower than his own.

When he asked who else I was interviewing, I mentioned Koehler trainer Tony Ancheta. The doctor flushed with anger, snatched Bill Koehler's book from his bookcase, and, contempt dripping, read Koehler's solution for correcting the dog who whines and/or barks in his owner's absence (what Dodman terms "separation anxiety"). "What disgusting bilge," Dodman said. "Helicoptering, hanging a dog, alpha rolls . . ."

I demurred. "There are some nutcases but I've never seen a respected trainer using those techniques."

"They are used all the time," the doctor corrected me.

Oh. O-kay.

Perhaps unwisely, I told Dr. Dodman about sheepdog Spot. Spot was a natural predator who dispatched possums and rabbits on sight. The skunk Spot killed didn't have time to loose her stink. When I took Spot into my small training ring, he shed a sheep and tried to pull her down by the throat.

I was readier for Spot's second lesson. When Spot and I walked into the ring, I carried a nylon stock whip.

This time, when Spot lunged for a ewe's throat, I cracked him across the withers. More shocked than hurt, the dog looked at me with sudden entire comprehension. Spot had had an epiphany — he, Spot, must not kill a sheep.

As I told Dr. Dodman, I never used a whip on a dog before nor afterwards and wouldn't recommend the stock whip as a routine training aide. Spot was a unique case and after that one lesson, Spot enjoyed a lengthy, happy life and never again tried to kill a sheep.

Dr. Dodman proclaimed, "I don't believe the end justifies the means."

"Do you know what happens to a sheep-killing dog on a sheep farm?"

The doctor pursed his lips.

Sleeping at my feet, June twitched and whimpered. I touched her gently to break the spell.

"She's just dreaming," Dodman informed me.

Dr. Dodman's interest in dogs began because his mother was "a neighborhood St. Francis of Assisi" and took in stray animals.

From rather vague early recollections, he segued into vivid memories of the boarding school he attended where punishments included being dragged by the ear and being smacked with a size-twelve sneaker. Caning — half a dozen blows across a boy's backside — was exquisitely painful.

"Can I see that," Dr. Dodman spoke in the voice of the boy he'd been. "And the victim would lower his pants to reveal rows of purple welts where he'd been struck." He added angrily, "There are laws against that sort of thing today."

I couldn't understand his point. Was Dr. Dodman equating traditional dog trainers with his schoolboy torments?

The doctor believes that "it is one medicine" for dogs and humans and that the similarity of dog and human DNA has produced crossover medical discoveries. Dodman writes: "Dogs can be thought of as having the same mental capacity as a three-year-old child — capable of simple communication, a good deal of affection, and an array of other emotions. They see the world as it is now, not the way it was a while back or how it will be in the future, and they want their rewards immediately."

Dr. Dodman enthuses about a Border Collie with a testable vocabulary of six hundred words.

But six hundred words isn't Shakespeare and Shakespeare couldn't tree a bear. I would like to meet the three-year-old human who could track and detain an escaped prisoner, swim across a tangled beaver bog to retrieve a wounded duck, work sheep a mile from its handler, or pull a dogsled eighteen hundred kilometers along the Iditarod.

However abusive it may have been, young Dodman's boarding school gave him excellent career advice: Nicholas Dodman was very good at science, pretty good in English, and okay at mathematics. His guidance counselor suggested a career in medicine.

Dr. Dodman wrinkles his nose at human medicine —"All those smelly feet"— and since Britain's National Health Service paid dentists piecework they worked themselves to death. "I preferred animals to people, and veterinary medicine was full of animals."

Before starting vet school he worked with a country vet "very much like James Herriot. We'd jump into the vet's Triumph and go haring down the road. Horses, donkeys, dogs: we saw them all." After vet school in Scotland he immigrated to Berkeley for his doctorate where he roomed with Ian Dunbar, an early positive training advocate. "Couldn't get Ian's face out of a book. He wouldn't come out for a beer."

Dodman pointed to a grab-and-grin photo of himself with Margaret Thatcher. "I left Britain because of Thatcher," he laughed. "Of course I didn't tell Thatcher that."

Dr. Dodman's specialty is obsessive-compulsive behaviors. In *Dogs Behaving Badly,* he writes:

> If susceptible humans under various forms of stress react by engaging in various compulsive behaviors related to their own species — typical orientations of grooming, exercising caution, gathering, and (arguably) hunting, why not dogs too? Dogs are self-groomers, predators, and imbibers (to name but a few of their naturalistic behaviors). Even from the drawing board one might expect some dogs to groom themselves compulsively when stressed: and they do. And you might expect others to compulsively chase things that are or are not there: they do this too. Or to drink water excessively when there is no known medical cause: they do. There are other conditions in dogs and across other domestic species that appear to confirm the view that compulsive behaviors are not unique to human beings but are also exhibited by animals.

Dr. Dodman treats lick granuloma (lesions caused by compulsive licking), tail-chasing, shadow-chasing, and thunderphobia, but he's best known for his work on "separation anxiety," a syndrome which many traditional trainers deny. Their disagreement infuriates Dr. Dodman. "If the symptoms are those of anxiety and the condition is treatable by anti-anxiety drugs, then it *is* separation anxiety. If it walks like a duck and quacks like a duck, it is a *duck!*"

June woke, stretched, and disappeared down the hall.

"You know," Dr. Dodman said, "only a small percentage of dogs are working dogs. Most people have pet dogs and they are family members. Why should such dogs learn to heel? They simply don't need it."

His client consultations take ninety minutes and he is available for phone follow-ups for six months.

Dr. Dodman was among the first veterinarians to prescribe (and publicize) psychoactive drugs for dogs.

I told him Luke had had a lick granuloma on his foot. "It's not the foot," Dr. Dodman said. "It's the head." He tapped his.

My vet prescribed an antibiotic for any underlying infection, a salve for the wound, and amitriptyline to enhance Luke's serotonin, which, Dr. Dodman writes, "is a modulator of central nervous system transmission and seems to have an effect on a tormented psyche like oil on the proverbial troubled waters."

Luke's sore healed. That's Good. But Luke stopped listening to me on the trial field. That's Bad.

Trialing is high stress. No mammalian brain is wired for so much intense concentration. The stressed-out trial dog's instincts may war with his training. He may quit contact with the sheep, run too wide — running, running, running — or he may lock up and lie there. Rarely, he'll even give up and leave the field. Not uncommonly he'll ignore his handler's increasingly frantic commands and take matters into his own paws.

The amitriptyline healed Luke's granuloma but he stopped listening to me on the trial fields and at Wendy Volhard's advice, I changed from once to twice daily feedings, added her Endurance nutritional supplement, and took Luke off the drug. Nowadays, Luke listens and his lick granuloma hasn't reappeared.

That amitripyline had had a negative side effect didn't interest Dr. Dodman.

We heard Ronni's surprised, "Well, and who are you!?" A moment later, she appeared in the doorway with June prancing at her side. "She's a lovely dog," Ronni said, holding a box of dog biscuits. "Can I give her a treat?"

"Just one."

June gave me a look. After her successful hustle, JUST ONE????

Dr. Dodman rolled his chair to the computer, brought up his web page, and showed me his accomplishments listed there.

In *The Well-Adjusted Dog* Dr. Dodman offers this opinion:

Some dogs growl — or worse — if you put your hand in their food bowl while they are eating. Dog trainers who use confrontational methods teach that you must be able to do this — that you have to make your dog tolerate this intervention to show him you're "alpha." This makes no sense to me at all. I know that I don't appreciate people sticking their hands in my food while I'm eating, and if a waiter did that to me in a restaurant, I would probably growl or snap at him. I can empathize with dogs in this situation and do not think they should have to tolerate such intrusion. My approach is to help owners appreciate that their dogs do not like their food touched while they are eating it, and I advise them not to do it.

Traditional trainers assert control of resources, especially food. Although my dogs don't beg at the table, sometimes after dinner, I'll set my plate on the floor and invite each of our six sheepdogs, in descending rank, to take a few licks before being replaced by the next lower ranked dog.

Dodman gave me a copy of his puppy-rearing book and I gave him *A Useful Dog.*

Her mission accomplished, June rejoined us.

"You know," Dr. Dodman said wistfully, "I never see well-behaved dogs in here. All the dogs I see have some sort of behavior problem."

Some Epiphanies

S INCE ROUNDING UP goats in West Texas last winter, Mr. and Mrs. Dog and I had put thirty thousand miles on the station wagon, from the Dakotas to New Hampshire to my calling June in on the wrong sheep at Gettysburg. That particular mistake knocked us out of the top seventeen, and walking off with a minute remaining (retired: score zero) might have bumped us off the United States Team. Sure, retiring spared June and the sheep — sixty seconds' worth. June and I had had a pretty good score until I quit.

Lucky for us, next year's National Finals Sheepdog Trials would be in South Dakota the exact same week as next year's World Trials, and transporting dog(s) to our Finals would be cheaper and miles easier than getting them to South Wales for the World.

For a century the Brits had maintained a six-month quarantine for dogs entering the UK. Six months. Six months in solitary confinement would drive most Border Collies insane. Literally. But once dogs could be microchipped and the Brits (sort of) joined the European Union, their Department of Environment, Food, and Rural Affairs (DEFRA) adopted a new protocol. Under the new rules, a US-microchipped dog could get a fresh rabies shot and have his blood tested by an EU-approved lab (in Kansas) to make sure the dog had rabies titers. Six months later it could enter the UK on a DEFRA-approved carrier.

Think of it as a six-month rabies quarantine (remote version).

June might still make the team but it'd be a while before I knew and DEFRA's paperwork was so formidable and the tickets so expensive I couldn't start without a go-ahead.

Cross my fingers and keep on trialing. June was running well but Luke wasn't. We'd solved his outrun problem — Luke would outrun for sheep he couldn't see — and we'd solved his pushiness problem with quieter but firmer whistles. Luke yearned to work brilliantly and was desperate to please. The more he hungered and the more I expected of him, the worse we did. I needed a wisdom fix and thought to get it from Bev Lambert.

Bev grew up without livestock experience and by sheer drive, commitment, and intelligence recreated herself as a brilliant sheepdog trainer and handler. Her day job was librarian. She must have been good at it because she regularly turned down raises: "Just give me extra time off so I can get away and trial." Some rough snuff-dippers Beverly routinely whipped at trials had threatened to visit her library to see Bev in her "work duds," but, far as I know, none ever made good on it.

Conditions on the Connecticut turnpike alternated between blinding snow and gobs of slush sixteen-wheelers tossed onto my road-salt-streaked windshield.

When I reached Beverly's farm, we couldn't do a thing. Ice-crusted snow made dangerous footing for dogs and sheep, so we drank coffee and chatted in her kitchen.

Beverly mentioned a scientific study investigating why some musical child prodigies go on to become successful adult musicians while others don't. They investigated variables: parental income and profession, education levels, and so forth. The only differential they found between those who made the grade and those who didn't, Bev said, was "hours practiced."

No doubt. But Luke and I had spent hundreds of hours training and we'd solved the big problems. He and I liked to train, we liked to work together, so why had he run out of gas when he got behind that wall at Gettysburg? Maybe ours hadn't been the right kind of practice.

I love music and regret not playing an instrument. As a child I took piano lessons and wasn't half bad. But my piano teacher didn't like me and I didn't like her and I hated the tunes I was assigned to play. Practice was drudgery, so that was that.

How does practice lead to mastery? Although I've driven many more hours than I've trained sheepdogs, if there was a United States Car-Driving Team I couldn't get on it. Mine hadn't been *correct* practice.

My dogs hate drill and will only put up with so much meaningless, repetitive work before they sour. Like us, they seem to learn best when asked to solve real problems: working at the limit of, but not beyond, their capacity. Their learning is subtle, almost cellular. Like Nile, the Labrador Retriever Behesha Doan trained, they react to cues so subtle the dogs themselves don't know they are being cued.

Sheepdogs think about their work. Trainers often crate the dog after a lesson so he can "think about" what he has learned and not have that lesson corrupted by fresher experience. If, for the first time, you've achieved a goal with your dog, you don't want to blur the lesson with excited ball play. As Tony Ancheta put it, after one week silently working the dog on a longe line, "you can relax and become an idiot again."

Not infrequently, the first time a young sheepdog is brought into a small ring with sheep he won't "see sheep." He'll amble around nibbling sheep poop, trying to interact with dogs outside the ring, or sucking up to his owner. If he's put up in a quiet place overnight though, next morning—without further input—he'll drop his tail and go into the sheepdog's predatory crouch. Though the dog doesn't understand what's happening to him, or that his genetics are busily expressing themselves, he knows he's doing SOMETHING and it's EXCITING and IMPORTANT—the biggest thing in his life.

But there's this man in the ring with him and the man blocks some of his moves and allows others. If he sulks the man cranks him up, and if he takes matters into his own paws, the man growls, threatens, slaps his cap against his leg, breaks his focus. We handlers are the sheepdog's longe line because we control access to the desirable sheep. As Jack Knox says, rolling his Scottish r's, "Allow the rrrright. Corrrrect the wrong."

Luke and June think and learn and respond to what they have learned but not exactly as I do. I have theories; they have method. Suppose, for instance, they're at Joanie Swanke's Dakota trial, where they'll outrun through alfalfa clumps for six hundred yards before they emerge suddenly, forty feet from five very spooky range Rambouillets. I, the handler, know there are range sheep out there and even know where they are. I know how undogged range Rambouillets react to dogs. I've walked the course and stood on that spot where my dog will first see the sheep. The dogs haven't been allowed on the course.

By human standards, I know far more than the dogs do. But Luke and June can do what I cannot. In a millisecond, forty feet from just-encountered range Rambouillets the dogs *see,* big as a Wall Drug bill board, which sheep is the leader. They immediately understand the complex social order in this particular miniflock. They know whether the sheep are ready to fight, split up, or break for the tall timber, because the sheep *tell* them what they mean to do. For the sake of that instant, for that millisecond, that's why the Mister and Missus have put so many miles beneath their paws. Luke and June have developed an all-sheep, all-breed, all-terrain method that doesn't give them an edge over dogs who've been working these sheep on this terrain all their lives, but does help them transmute the novel into the manageable.

On January 25 I learned June was on the United States Team for the World Trial. On February 14, I learned I could bring a second dog. Mrs. Dog had bought her ticket, Luke's ticket, and my ticket too.

Ethology

JOE MAZEROS was the finest practical ethologist I've ever known. He escaped from Hungary during the 1956 revolution and claimed he descended from a long line of successful poachers. How could he know they were successful? "In Hungary, the penalty for poaching was castration."

Last fall we'd planted alfalfa in our riverside field, but it hadn't established a stand. Our farm routinely feeds deer, but come April the deer infestation was serious, and when a deer eats the crown of a young alfalfa plant it dies.

The game warden gave me a permit to shoot five deer with a restriction: we couldn't kill bucks. That restriction made me uneasy. The does had very young fawns on them and though I didn't object to a quick death for the doe, I was troubled by the subsequent starvation of her unmothered fawn.

The last time we had a permit, we invited neighbors to spotlight nuisance deer. Mesmerized by a spotlight, deer are easy targets. The hunters who showed up at two in the morning cut deep tire ruts in our field and didn't pick up the one deer they killed because they were too drunk to find it.

This time I asked Joe for help. He said, "Wait until the full moon. Do not worry. I won't shoot a doe with a fawn on her.

"When deer are spotlighted it is alien to their experience. Spotlighting is like lightning — an unrepeatable natural disaster. Excepting the deer that was killed, tomorrow night they will return to their preferred graze. I will slip down there and shoot one doe and let her lie until morning. Next night, I'll shoot another. The deer will think, 'Horrors! This is where Hazel died. And Ethel too.' And they'll shun your alfalfa field."

He did. They did. I asked Joe how he knew he was shooting barren does. "They were fat. No fawns to pull them down."

Although it's hard to think of ethology without thinking of Konrad Lorenz, he wasn't the first ethologist. That honor belonged to an anonymous Paleolithic hunter waiting at a waterhole for his prey.

Lorenz credited his teacher Oskar Heinroth, "who was most careful to describe animal behavior as objectively as possible. . . . [He] was often accused by animal lovers of misrepresenting living creatures as being machines, because of his mechanistic interpretations of behavior. To such aspersions he used to answer: 'Quite the contrary. I regard animals as very emotional people with very little intelligence!'"

It was Heinroth who discovered imprinting (the instinct that can make a baby goose believe a human is its mother). His pupil Lorenz made much of this discovery. Lorenz and his great friend Nickolass Tinbergen refined and popularized ethology.

Tinbergen wrote:

> In 1936 Van der Klaauw invited Konrad Lorenz to Leiden for a small symposium on "Instinct," and it was then that Konrad and I first met. We "clicked" at once. The Lorenzes invited us, with our small son, for a four months' stay in their parental home in Altenberg near Vienna, where I became Lorenz' second pupil (the first being Dr. Alfred Seitz, of the *Seitz's Reizsummenregel*). But from the start "pupil" and "master" influenced each other. Konrad's extraordinary vision and enthusiasm were supplemented and fertilized by my critical sense, my inclination to think his ideas through, and my irrepressible urge to check our "hunches" by experimentation — a gift for which he had an almost childish admiration. Throughout this we often burst into bouts of hilarious fun — in Konrad's words, in *Lausbuberei* [rascaliness].
>
> These months were decisive for our future collaboration and our lifelong friendship.

Lorenz and Tinbergen made a great team. As Richard Burkhardt writes:

> Tinbergen provided Lorenz with more than experimental support. He was a clearer, more analytical thinker than was his much more intuitive Austrian colleague. . . . Besides their very different intellectual styles, the two men differed in their personalities. Tinbergen was self-deprecating, reflective,

inclined to feel guilty if he had been enjoying himself, and prepared to listen to other points of view. Lorenz was egoistic, impulsive, happy to enjoy himself, and disposed to be angry when criticized. They also differed in their cherished scientific practices. As Lorenz described it, he in his own work was by nature a farmer. Tinbergen, in contrast, was a hunter. Lorenz liked raising and breeding animals, nurturing them when they were ill, and having them as companions. Tinbergen preferred stalking animals in the field, matching wits with them, and discovering how the details of their behavior contributed to their survival.

Although Lorenz joined the Nazi Party and toyed with notions of racial purity, he and Tinbergen remained friends until Tinbergen was imprisoned for protesting the Nazification of Leiden University.

Lorenz was conscripted and sent as a doctor to the Russian front where he disappeared.

After the war, Tinbergen refused to meet German scientists but was ecstatic when he learned Lorenz had survived as a Russian POW. He later wrote: "Our reunion, in 1949, in the hospitable home of W. H. Thorpe in Cambridge, was to both of us a deeply moving occasion."

In 1963, Tinbergen defined the questions ethology asked of a particular behavior:

1. What is its survival value? (The clear submission/dominance signals dogs send each other prevent fighting.)

2. What is its evolutionary history? (They send these signals because their ancestors were cooperative hunters and had to work together.)

3. What are the cause and effect relations that underlie it? (Border Collies are bred to be compulsive workers. This is good when they have work to do. Without it, they express their compulsiveness in objectionable ways.)

4. What is the individual history of the animal? (Poorly socialized pups are harder to train. Pups removed from their mother too young and before she starts teaching canine manners may have difficulty understanding other dogs' cues.)

Ethology is profoundly evolutionary and favors nature over nurture.

Curiously, ethology, which performed few "controlled" and "quantifiable" experiments and didn't fret about whether it was a science or not, has had a better reception among hard scientists than behaviorism.

In *On Aggression,* Lorenz began developing a concept of drives. Here's how he distinguishes between fight (defense) and prey drives: "The buffalo which the lion fells provokes his aggression as little as the appetizing turkey which I have just seen hanging in the larder provokes mine. The difference in these inner drives can clearly be seen in the expressive movements of the animal: a dog about to catch a hunted rabbit has the same kind of excitedly happy expression as he has when he greets his master or awaits some longed-for treat."

Ethologists often argue for behavioral complexity. Most pet owners see dog play as simple, happy, perhaps puppyish exuberance. Sorry folks, 'tain't that simple . . . In their 1990 *Wolf Ethogram,* Pat Goodman and Erich Klinghammer describe wolf "play":

> A "playing wolf"—in fact many other canids as well—performs what has been called the "play bow." . . . However, at Wolf Park, we have wolf-bison demonstrations each Sunday during our open season. Since the bison are all healthy, they show no fear of the wolves and charge them when they come too close during the demonstrations. The wolves typically approach the bison and bow while intently observing the bison. They will dash forward, jump back or to either side, when the bison charges. One would be hard-pressed to interpret the wolves' bow posture as an invitation to "play" with the bison. This bowing—the "play bow"—is instead a position the wolf adopts whenever it does not know what will happen next. . . .
>
> We think this same kind of testing takes place among pack members who know each other well. The "play bow" in social interactions looks playful to the uninitiated because nothing serious is happening. Despite this seemingly friendly behavior, the wolves are, in fact, constantly testing each other. When one wolf sees an opening for whatever reason, the "play" changes instantly into an attack.

My sheep-guarding dogs don't like "their" sheep used for sheepdog training but know they must not interfere. A sheepdog appears suddenly running toward "their" sheep. If it is an inexperienced or unknown dog the guarding dogs intervene. If the sheepdog is familiar and "trusted" the guarding dogs allow the sheepdog to fetch the sheep, while they run and play like huge puppies out in front of "their" flock. Their play is, I believe, stress relief.

My sheepdog Pip had conflicted maternal feelings. If Pip didn't return when sent into the lambing field, I'd look until I found him and the distressed/separated/entangled lamb he was guarding. When we had a fading orphan lamb, a lamb we'd tried to revive without success, as a last resort we'd intubate it with warm milk replacer, carry it indoors, and lay it on a sheepskin beside the woodstove. Pip would "mother" the lamb, licking and cleaning it. Yes, he saved a few. But it was obvious, watching Pip, that he was torn between nurturing the precious creature and killing and eating it.

Lorenz writes:

> A definite and self-contained function of an organism, such as feeding, copulation, or self-preservation, is never the result of a single cause or of a single drive.... The everyday, common, "cheap" fixed motor patterns which I have called the "little servants of species preservation" are often at the disposal of more than one of the "big" drives. Particularly the behavior patterns of locomotion, such as running, flying, swimming, etc., also those of pecking, gnawing and digging can be used in the service of feeding, reproduction, flight and aggression, which we will here call the "big drives." Because the little servants play a subsidiary part of "common final path-ways" to various super systems, in particular to the above mentioned "big four," I have called them tool activities. This, however, does not mean that such motor patterns lack their own spontaneity. On the contrary, it is compatible with a widespread principle of natural economy that, for example in a dog or a wolf, the spontaneous production of the separate impulses of sniffing, tracking, running, chasing and shaking to death is roughly adapted to the demands of hunger. If we exclude hunger as a motive, by the simple method of keeping the dish full, it will soon be noticed that the animal sniffs, tracks, runs and chases hardly less than when these activities are necessary to allay its hunger. Still, if the dog is very hungry, he does all this qualitatively more. Thus, though the tool instincts possess their own spontaneity, they are driven, in this case by hunger, to perform more than they would if left alone. Indeed, a drive can be driven.

Drive theory informs contemporary Schutzhund, protection dog, and retriever training. It underpins influential pet dog tests and training practices.

Drives

Drive-trained dogs are very much more reliable.
—Wendy Volhard

NOW THAT WE actually were on the United States Team, I needed to face the alarming forms that would allow me and the Mister and Missus into Britain. I had to involve my vet and figure travel arrangements.

Instead, we three played hooky.

When Wendy Volhard and her dogs crossed the bridge into the meadow she wasn't happy to meet Luke and June. "I certainly hope those dogs are trained to off-leash standard," she said. Her small Labrador (mix?) was on lead, but two small terriers weren't and rushed Luke and June. "Hi! Hi! Hi! Call me Julie!"

June's hackles raised — must she put these brash dogs in their places? — but she and Luke accepted their attentions stoically, if not enthusiastically. Border Collies are racists and though they recognize that other dog breeds exist they expect them to ride in the back of the bus.

Wendy Volhard is thin and athletic and speaks with a slight British accent in complete sentences and paragraphs. With her husband, Jack, she has authored nine training books. Her recent books include *Dog Training for Dummies* and (without Jack) a treatise on holistic pet nutrition, *Holistic Guide for a Healthy Dog*. The Volhards' puppy test is the gold standard for evaluating puppies, and the couple has been developing their motivational training method for nearly forty years. Luke, June, and I were visiting their thirty-second dog trainer camp.

The brash Terriers and stoic Border Collies were already ignoring each other. Apologizing for her asperity, Wendy explained that all levels of dogs attended the camp; some dogs were untrained and unreliable off-leash.

The headquarters and guest quarters of Graves' Mountain Lodge sprawled along a steep ridge above the ten-acre riverside meadow where a tennis court, volleyball court, and horseshoe pegs were disused and forlorn. It was early April and the lodge had just opened for the season.

It was beautiful, this valley beneath the Blue Ridge. Spring grass was luxuriant and I could probably have drunk from the clear river running through the place (though not after the Labradors had their retrieving lesson). As I drove to the main lodge to check in, Jack Volhard and blue-jacketed assistants were unpacking agility and obedience equipment.

TWENTY YEARS AGO, Wendy Volhard attended a seminar in Buffalo, New York, that, she says in all seriousness, "changed her life." In Europe, some of Konrad Lorenz's pupils had elaborated on his drive theory to train Schutzhund (protection) dogs. At that Buffalo seminar, the German instructor worked his demonstration shepherd silently with body language so subtle it was hard for experienced trainers to see what he was doing.

"It was poetry to watch this man command 'bite,' 'back off'... all without a word," Wendy recalled. "He was brilliant with the dogs but terrible with people. He told everybody their dog was worthless."

Maybe Wendy's German Shepherd Katharina wasn't worthless or maybe the instructor realized he'd made a human relations blunder because he blurted an explanation: "These dogs don't have enough defense drive!"

"Defense drive?" Wendy puzzled.

Next morning, after a hearty breakfast, the dog trainers and I adjourned to a pine-paneled conference room for an introduction to Volhard methodology and a quiz intended to individuate each dog's training. Courtesy of the Volhards, here's the test. You might take it yourself.

Canine Personality Profile

To help you understand how to approach your dog's training, we developed Volhard's Personality Profile for each dog. The profile catalogs ten behaviors in each drive that influence the dog's responses and which are useful to us in training. The ten behaviors chosen are those that most closely represent the strengths of the dog in each of the drives. The profile does not pretend to include all behaviors seen in a dog, nor the complexity of their interaction. Although it is an admittedly crude index of your dog's behavior, you will find it surprisingly accurate.

The results of the profile will give you a better understanding of why your dog is the way he is and the most successful way to train him. You can then make use of his strengths, avoid needless confusion, and greatly reduce the time it takes to train him.

Evaluating the Profile

When completing the profile, keep in mind that it was devised for a house dog or pet with an enriched environment, perhaps even a little training, and not a dog tied out in the yard or kept solely in a kennel—such dogs have fewer opportunities to express as many behaviors as a house dog. Answers should indicate those behaviors your dog would exhibit if he had not already been trained to do otherwise. For example, did he jump on people to greet them, or jump on the counter to steal food, before he was trained not to do so?

The fight part of the defense drive does not fully express itself until the dog is mature, around two to four years of age, depending on the breed, although you may see tendencies toward those behaviors earlier.

Young dogs tend to exhibit more flight behaviors than older dogs.

The Questionnaire

The questionnaire for the profile suggests three possible answers to each question with a corresponding point value. The possible answers and their corresponding values are:

Almost always—10
Sometimes—5
Hardly ever—0

For example, if your dog is a Beagle, the answer to the question "When presented with the opportunity, does your dog sniff the ground or air?" is probably "Almost always," giving him a score of 10.

You may not have had the chance to observe all of these behaviors, in which case you leave the answer blank.

When presented with the opportunity:

1. Does YOUR DOG sniff the ground or air a lot?
2. Does YOUR DOG get along with other dogs?
3. Does YOUR DOG stand its ground or investigate strange objects or sounds?
4. Does YOUR DOG run away from new situations?
5. Does YOUR DOG get excited by moving objects, such as bikes or squirrels?
6. Does YOUR DOG get along with people?
7. Does YOUR DOG like to play tug of war games to win?
8. Does YOUR DOG hide behind you when unable to cope?
9. Does YOUR DOG stalk cats, other dogs, or things in the grass?
10. Does YOUR DOG bark when left alone?
11. Does YOUR DOG bark or growl in a deep tone?
12. Does YOUR DOG act fearful in unfamiliar situations?
13. Does YOUR DOG, when excited, bark in a high-pitched voice?
14. Does YOUR DOG solicit petting or like to snuggle with you?
15. Does YOUR DOG guard territory?
16. Does YOUR DOG tremble or whine when unsure?
17. Does YOUR DOG pounce on his toys?
18. Does YOUR DOG like to be groomed?
19. Does YOUR DOG guard food or toys?
20. Does YOUR DOG crawl or turn upside down when reprimanded?
21. Does YOUR DOG shake and "kill" toys?
22. Does YOUR DOG seek eye contact with you?
23. Does YOUR DOG dislike being petted?
24. Is YOUR DOG reluctant to come close to you when called?
25. Does YOUR DOG steal food or garbage?

26. Does YOUR DOG follow you around like a shadow?
27. Does YOUR DOG dislike being groomed or bathed?
28. Does YOUR DOG have difficulty standing still when groomed?
29. Does YOUR DOG like to carry things?
30. Does YOUR DOG play a lot with other dogs?
31. Does YOUR DOG guard the owner(s)?
32. Does YOUR DOG cringe when someone strange bends over him/her?
33. Does YOUR DOG wolf down food?
34. Does YOUR DOG jump up to greet people?
35. Does YOUR DOG like to fight with other dogs?
36. Does YOUR DOG urinate during greeting behavior?
37. Does YOUR DOG like to dig and bury things?
38. Does YOUR DOG show reproductive behaviors, such as courting or mounting other dogs?
39. Does YOUR DOG get picked on by other dogs (either now or when it was young)?
40. Does YOUR DOG tend to bite when cornered?

Scoring the Profile

1.	2.	3.	4.
5.	6.	7.	8.
9.	10.	11.	12.
13.	14.	15.	16.
17.	18.	19.	20.
21.	22.	23.	24.
25.	26.	27.	28.
29.	30.	31.	32.
33.	34.	35.	36.
37.	38.	39.	40.
Total prey drive	Total pack drive	Total fight drive	Total flight drive

Although I dutifully scored Luke and June, there were difficulties. If a dog has never had a toy, what score for "tearing toys apart"? If they have never snatched food, how to score abstemious dogs?

While other trainers were happily claiming prey and pack scores in the high nineties, Luke earned an anemic 45 and June's highest score in any category was a sorry 35. Luke's sorting off and dis-earing sheep did earn 10 prey drive bonus points.

Wendy said, "Have you ever noticed the first thing your dog does when he comes out in the morning? He looks around and sniffs the air. That's prey drive, which is stimulated by seeing, smelling, and hearing. Prey drive is dangerous because out of prey drive comes killing."

Prey drive bad. Sorry, Luke.

The fight drive "indicates a dog's self-confidence in stressful situations. A dog with a strong fight drive stands his ground." Luke's crate defense when a stranger gets too near produced 5 more bonus points.

Pack drive "determines our relations with the dog. When you're asking for maximum cooperation, you're in pack drive."

Defense: "When a dog has low defense drive, he's stressed all the time. But it's a premium for training. To get from prey to pack drive, you must go through defense."

TO HELP TRAIN these newly drive-calibrated dogs, the Top Dog Camp has eight assistants. Counting Wendy and Jack Volhard there's an instructor for every four participants.

I visited the "Fast Track" class intended for novices with beginner dogs and experienced trainers improving basic training techniques.

In one part of a covered pavilion, instructors fitted collars on the dogs: plastic choke collars for dogs with low defense scores and prong collars (aka the "religious" collar) for dogs "high in defense."

Each dog would be trained daily, and Wendy warned her students: "While under ordinary circumstances, your dog may be a perfect angel, he or she is not used to being trained three to four hours a day. It has been our experience that on the afternoon of the third day, the dogs become a little tired and sometimes irritable, so that special vigilance is required.

Incidentally, you may experience similar feelings by the afternoon of only the second day. Should this happen to you, take a break."

On the other side of the pavilion, an instructor was teaching advanced handlers the correct footwork for AKC obedience heeling exercises. Without dogs, students stepped off as precisely as a Prussian drill team while the instructor commanded "Right turn," "Left turn," and "About turn."

In the meadow, Wendy Volhard taught the broad jump ("It's a rule of dogs. The faster the dog moves, the slower the handler must") while Jack Volhard taught advanced obedience. Exiting the agility tunnel, dogs paused to hoover treats earlier dogs had missed.

A kindly student offered June a treat. June thought it was okay but nothing to write home about.

At dinner that evening, I sat beside a trainer's husband who didn't give a hoot about dogs: he was a World War II reenactor.

"Oh," I said.

He and his fellow reenactors fought battles whenever they could get enough Yanks and Nazis together. It was hard to arrange air cover. Vintage WWII aircraft are terrible gas hogs.

"What about tanks?" I asked.

He assured me tanks were no problem. After the war ended, many surviving Panther and Tiger tanks had been buried as bunkers on the Czech border. Now they were being dug up, so you could buy a perfectly good Nazi tank on eBay.

I'd spent two years training and trialing my dogs. I'd sought enlightenment from the best dog trainers in the country. I'd put thirty-four thousand miles on a twenty-year-old station wagon.

In the fall I'd fly two dogs to Paris, cross the channel, and cross Britain to Wales to compete in the longest shot of my life.

Buying tanks on eBay? Why not? Made perfect sense to me.

A Thousand Yards

I T'S EASIER (and cheaper) to squeeze a camel through the eye of a needle than to fly two forty-five pound dogs to Britain. DEFRA-approved air carriers accepted dogs as cargo, US to the UK, at $860 one way. Per dog. Plus kennel costs in the UK and the owner's ticket and expenses over there. It looked like $4,000–$5,000.

Or I could fly to Paris (my ticket plus $600 round trip for both dogs as excess baggage) and enter the UK on the DEFRA-approved Calais/Dover ferry ($150 round trip). Hmmm.

Our trip must satisfy three sets of regulations: the French, DEFRA, and the International Air Travel Association (IATA). Make one mistake and the Mister and Missus would be turned back at the port of entry. At the previous World Trials several Americans were turned back, and the return flight was so expensive Scott Glenn had to sell one dog to get himself and the other dog home.

I didn't know which rule might safely be ignored; prudence suggested I cross every T.

Hence, I assumed when a form asked for military (24 hour) time, they meant 1310 not ten past one. When the IATA suggested ventilated crates two sizes larger than Luke and June ever traveled in, I bored extra air holes in two huge (11 cubic feet each) Vari Kennel 500 dog crates.

My vet patiently filled out umpteen forms, which I stored in their own blue file folder. Three weeks before we were to leave, DEFRA updated their microchips. The Mister and Missus carried "old-fashioned" chips and every form was tied to their microchipped doggy IDs.

As it happened I could rent a microchip scanner. "Yes, Mister Port-of-Entry Official, sir. If your machine can't read my microchips, this here reader can!" I rented one.

Although the French forms were identical to the Brit forms they were in FRENCH. Could I trust French officials not to get weird? Had they forgiven us "freedom fries"?

So my vet filled out French forms too and I made a second five-hour drive to the USDA office in Richmond to get them stamped and — for the hell of it — I had them stamp an international health certificate although nobody had told me I needed one.

I don't like to fly dogs. I've heard too many horror stories. But, I confess, I've never had a problem and the airline people I met must have had dogs of their own. In San Antonio, after our flight was cancelled, the ticket agent rescued June from the baggage room so she and I could wait in the airport dog park. On a rainy morning in Charlottesville, the gate agent said, "We're backed up in Atlanta and might get the 'go' call anytime. But I'll unload your dogs and we'll take our chances."

But under the best of conditions, flying dogs is a pain in the ass.

Primed to worry every bit as much as they can, War on Terror thinkers have moved parking garages away from airport terminals. Luggage carts in the parking garage? Lots of luck. Porters? You must be joking.

For domestic flights, I put wheels on one ordinary-size dog crate, bungee-cord a second crate atop it, slide my luggage into the crates, and clip the Mister and Missus to string leads.

Wearing an "I know what I'm doing" expression on my homely phiz, I blow past the "All dogs must be crated" sign and beeline for the ticket desk.

Should a TSA person try to intercept me, I don't slow to argue but cry, "They haven't been through SECURITY."

My invocation of the Magic Word freezes the person's brain just long enough for me to get to the ticket counter where I check my luggage, remove crate wheels, and settle Luke and June into the crates — after they've been patted down by security.

I couldn't pull that stunt with Air France at Dulles. Just another thing to worry about.

The hell with the worries. Working the Mister and Missus settles my nerves.

At important trials, the sheep might be set out eight hundred, nine hundred, even a thousand yards from the handler's post. At some it takes the dog four minutes to get behind his sheep and at those distances, my whistle reaches the dog's ears two seconds after I whistle it.

Two weeks before our departure for Wales, the third cutting came off Steve McCall's big field in southwest Virginia and the dogs and I drove down for our final practice.

The Henrys' house sits on a hilltop where the sunrise is saluted by a neighbor's rooster. Luke and June sniffed and pursued the scent trails of the Henrys' dogs.

David and Christine Henry loaded a dozen Katahdin sheep and an ATV into a stock trailer and I followed on narrow country roads until we turned in past a big antebellum plantation house and dairy barns, up a rough farm track to the big field.

From one end to the other, the big field's a mile; at its widest, half a mile. It's an uneven rectangle downhill and up again to the ridge that bounds it. I was on one ridge; David and Christine were on the other. The rising sun was in my eyes.

I did see a human silhouette on the far ridge. I thought I could see David's ATV. The sheep were over there somewhere.

The radio crackled. "You ready?"

"Aaa-waaay to me . . ."

June disappeared into a gully. Perhaps David could spot her. "What's she doing?"

"She's by the round baler; looks like she's going to crossover."

June took a redirect whistle (one point deduction at a trial), but she found, gathered, and brought her sheep. Luke-the-blockhead decided that five hundred yards wasn't where I really, really, REALLY wanted him to look for sheep, so he ran out, perfectly, to the farthest fence: a full mile.

Oh shit.

A mile away, Luke was a flyspeck on a flyspeck that disappeared for minutes at a time. Thank God for the radios: David told me, "He's in the bottom."

Then, "He's on the back fence beside the corn."

It should have been easy to direct Luke to the sheep. He was on the far side and a simple recall should have brought him to them.

You think?

Luke returned to me after making an incredibly long outrun and searching but never finding any sheep. Bad. Very bad.

Too clearly I recalled Luke's history. I really, really hoped he didn't. I prayed he'd forgotten that terrible day at the Bloomfield trial where young Luke learned there were no sheep out there for him to find — no matter how he tried — and his trusted handler was yelling at him.

Luke's eyes were big and keen and honest.

"What's going on in there, Luke?" I asked. "What's going on in that walnut-sized brain?"

Luke wagged — a little wearily.

David got on the radio. "You gonna send him again?"

If Luke didn't find them this second time — if he ran out all that way and found no sheep again — would he be willing to go out in Wales? Would he trust me?

Luke said he could do it. Together, we'd traveled so very many hours, so many miles. Partner, we've seen some things, haven't we? If he couldn't trust me, who could he trust?

He cocked himself like a pistol.

"Come by."

Luke sped away, over a hummock out of sight, THERE HE IS FOR AN EYEBLINK . . . gone again . . .

So I wait. I remember to breathe. In through the nose, out through the mouth. There's a hawk circling in the blue morning air.

David's on the radio. "He's behind them. He's got the sheep."

I sag and take a deep breath. Well now. Well now. I won't need to cancel Luke's reservation after all.

Four minutes and twenty seconds after he left my feet the Mister *did* pick up his sheep. And, you bet, he brought them directly to me.

Piece of cake. Nothing to it.

One More River to Cross

If they don't want us to come, why don't they just say so?
— Chuck Dimit, United States Team

I'D FORGOTTEN one teensy-weensy detail. The last thing one does before flying dogs to the UK is get a tick treatment (Advantix preferred) and a tapeworm pill (must contain praziquantel), which your vet *must* administer twenty-four hours but not forty-eight hours before the dog is accepted at the port of entry. My vet did so at exactly 1608 EDT, 27 August.

What with calculating EDT (eastern daylight), CEST (central European summer), and BST (British standard) time zones, I'd forgotten Air France, which would fly Luke, June, and moi from Dulles: check-in at 1345 EDT, 28 August, takeoff at 1645 EDT same date.

My vet had filled out and stamped the tick/tapeworm certificate. His tech had dutifully noted the date (dd/mm/yyyy) and time (24 hour clock), *but* I would be checking my dogs in with Air France twenty-one hours after the injection, which is not twenty-four hours.

It takes a worried man. I dithered. I made contingency plans. I cleaned up: shaved, donned dress pants, blazer, and tie. I exuded confidence. Should some Air France functionary note the time and cry, "Non, Monsieur!," I'd demand to see his supervisor and browbeat the man into agreeing that going by TAKEOFF time instead of CHECK-IN time my dogs met that twenty-four hour test . . .

That's how it is, friends. Traveling with dogs makes you nuts.

I'd installed the required crate pads and waterers in each huge plastic crate. My duffle bulged with all-weather clothing, rain suit, wellies, meds, the dog bag (don't forget the flashlight! Don't forget the anti-stress supplement!). My carry-on held a rented cellphone, iBook, GPS (loaded with a French and British flash memory card), camera, precious blue file folder, numerous chargers/adapters, my rented microchip scanner, shooting glasses, and two books — Alters's *The David Story* and Alastair McLeod's *Island*. I burn through mediocre books. These two should outlast this adventure.

Each huge *verdammt* crate with a forty-five-pound dog inside took two men to lift. The Dulles Airport porter slid them onto his cart and wheeled briskly to Air France, where I handed my passport and ticket to an authoritative woman who gestured at the dogs: "I must see their papers."

Oh shit! Here's where — because of an imperfectly timed *tick shot* — they turn us away: No World Trial/End of Story.

My blue folder contained an impressive array of papers: one six-page form in English with its six-page mate in French (both APHIS certified) for each dog, plus confirmations for US motels, Air France, French car rental, P&O ferry, Dover B&B, International Sheepdog Society (ISDS) forms, dog pedigrees, Brit car rental, Carmarthen B&B . . .

I gave the agent the international health certificate: the form everyone assured me I wouldn't need. She examined it, ripped off the top copy, smiled, and directed me to security. SHE DIDN'T EVEN ASK TO SEE THE TICK AND TAPES FORM!

TSA minions ordered me to lie Luke and June down and roll each dog onto its back so they could confirm neither had an explosive belt on its doggy undercarriage. After which they lost interest. I left the dogs with them. The dogs said, "Oh no! Not Another Airplane!" with their eyes.

After more of the pointless humiliations we air travelers endure I boarded a shuttle to the departure terminal. And since I was presently fret-free, I dug deep for a fresh fret.

After his last domestic flight, Luke arrived with a note taped to his crate: "Caution! Cross Dog! Watch your fingers!" Luke's never bitten anyone, but he doesn't like strangers jostling his crate. At Atlanta Hartsfield a couple years back, June and Luke were being transferred from big plane to tiny when the baggage man came over where I was watching. "Is that your dog? He seems upset."

He reversed the conveyor, Luke descended, and I told Luke to chill. Luke chilled.

Not everyone is as sensible as that baggage man. Some folks hear one growl and freak: "Dangerous dog!" Airlines won't carry dangerous dogs.

As I boarded the plane, I asked the steward to tell me when my dogs were aboard. On tenterhooks, I waited for bad news.

A very long twenty minutes later the steward told me my dog was on board.

"I have *two* dogs."

"Oui, Monsieur. Both are on board."

Okay. OKAY! I peeled off my blazer and stuffed the damn thing in the overhead. I untied my tie.

I never did find out what the movie was.

ELEVEN HOURS, twenty minutes later (CEST), Luke and June emerged with the odd-lot luggage in terminal D2, Charles de Gaulle Aéroport, Paris.

CDG had no porters, but a luggage cart was provided that would have been perfectly adequate for the standard suitcase and carry-on but was woefully inadequate for us. I let June out and she stretched. June said, "Wooo." I set her crate crossways on the cart and asked her to crate up. I unloaded Luke who said, "Hello, hello." "Yes, Lukey, hello." I balanced his crate atop June's and invited him to leap into it, which he did. Cart and crates were taller than I am.

My left elbow is arthritic, and my right rotator cuff had recently been smashed between a ram and the hard ground. I eyed my seventy-five-pound duffle until I morphed into Super Geezer. Yes, the damn thing was heavy and yes, I was battered, old, and out of shape. But how many tens of thousands of seventy-five-pound hay bales had I bucked into one barn loft or another? Big goddamn deal!

Without further ado I bucked the duffle atop the stack.

Two big dog crates, dogs, and a fat duffle on those puny cart wheels: pure ridiculosity. Couldn't be helped.

I adjusted my Stetson to the proper John Wayne angle (late John Wayne — his Rooster Cogburn period), hung my carry-on on the handles, and, peering around it so I wouldn't bang into anybody, navigated my contraption past citizens of France's former African colonies dressed in finely wrought lace and cotton dashikis. Through passport control — no dog papers demanded — down another long hall, altering direction cautiously, a bit at a time, so the mad shebang (including Luke and June) wouldn't topple over.

WHEN I BORE DOWN on the rental car agent he blurted, "You need a bigger car."

He gave me keys for a Citroen minivan which was buried in space 266 in terminal D2's rental car park. There may be worse car parks. Picture an airshaft plummeting into a grease pit. Far overhead, I *could* see the sky. Cars whipped past my contraption with Gallic insouciance.

Out of traffic behind my rental, I jumped the Mister and Missus out for a quick pee. They thanked me.

My "big" Citroen was much smaller than a Ford Explorer. I could just jam one huge crate into it so I broke the other one down. June could ride in the stack while Luke sat in the passenger seat. The rest of my gear stowed wherever.

I adjusted the mirrors, fastened my seatbelt, turned on my GPS, and fired up the engine. The car started but the GPS didn't. Okay, I'm in a deep hole well below satellite notice. Right? Right???

Wrong. As I exited the airport under clear blue satellite-littered skies my GPS kept mum. Another damned Francophobe! Without GPS guidance I was speeding out of the busiest airport in Europe without map, directions, or the faintest idea where I was going.

Despite disapproving Gallic horns, I veered into the cab rank of the airport Hilton and dashed inside where the concierge advised me to turn toward Lille. "Just beyond the Concorde."

An actual, real Concorde was mounted beside the road on a plinth like a child's airplane model. The Concorde was bigger than that model but smaller than I'd imagined.

Fifty kilometers down the A20 I pulled around back of a truck stop so Luke and June could poop among Gallic trash and weeds. They drank a bowl of Evian water.

I passed signs for French cathedrals, battlefields, and castles but couldn't stop because my body was snarling, "Yo Fool! It's three in the morning! EDT! How about a little snoozeroo?"

If I stopped I'd sleep, and then I'd miss my ferry and the forty-eight-hour tick treatment deadline.

Calais was an English holiday town: French and British flags everywhere. The ancien régime café rubbed elbows with an Irish pub. I shunned the "Australian pizza" in favor of a local specialty: moules frites (mussels and chips). In retrospect, I should have chanced the pizza.

Since Luke and June would be back in crates for the Dover ferry I took them to the beach to stretch out, but a sign declared "No dogs between May 15 and October 15" and there were too many damn beach police. Some stretch-out: the Mister and Missus on string leads and grumpy Donald behind them.

With Luke and June snoozing at my feet, I killed a couple hours in a beachfront café drinking espresso and watching enormous P&O ferries in and out of Calais harbor. Some carried ten lanes of cars on each of three decks.

According to the P&O website, foot passengers must check in an hour before sailing. The website didn't mention the entire absence of parking near the terminal nor zip-shit shuttle buses to transport one, one's dogs, one's crates, and one's duffle the half mile to the ticket counter.

It was a slog. With June at my heel I dragged her 500 crate into the lobby and she got in it. Then I delivered Luke and 500 number 2.

When I crated Luke and turned to go back for my duffle and carry-on, a ticket agent huffily instructed, "Monsieur cannot leave his luggage unattended."

I was tired and peeved. I said, "The dogs will guard it."

"Dogs, Monsieur? Dogs? Monsieur . . ."

I left without answering her.

When I reappeared with the rest of my gear, the agent was on the phone with a supervisor. She forgot about unattended dog-guarded luggage and hurried me and my file folder through locked gates topped with razor wire. We were buzzed through to a security tower where her supervisor apologized: "We don't get many walk-on dogs. One or two in a year."

The supervisor was friendly and competent but didn't relax the rules. On his fingers, he ticked off forty-four hours, adjusted for eastern daylight to central European summer time, from when our vet had treated Luke and June for tick and tapes. More than twenty-four hours, less than forty-eight. The supervisor filled out more forms and stamped them.

I dragged the 500s and duffle through passport control into a departure lounge. The Mister and Missus trotted alongside and June greeted her first gendarme.

The dogs sat with me until near departure time when hordes of British holiday-makers crammed the room with strollers and shrieking toddlers. Back in the crates again.

I was fretting how we'd get my menagerie aboard the ferry when a miraculous minibus appeared. Luke and June perched on the seat, peering out the window at enormous articulated lorries and rows of cars on a gray, drizzly pier. What did they think? What was going on in their doggy minds?

The bus dropped into the ferry's lower deck, echoing with roaring motors, clattering steel plates, and ferrymen's bellowed instructions. Dog accommodation was a steel mesh cage into which went the Mister and Missus, their 500s, and my duffle. I couldn't meet the dogs' eyes as I abandoned them again.

I took an elevator to the lounge for a very stiff drink. The lounge was loud with beeping, blinking gambling machines and many extremely jolly tourists. The English Channel was pea-soup fog.

Next thing I knew, someone was shaking my shoulder.

Back down to the dog cage. Cars and lorries were clattering aboard for the return. I told a ferryman I really didn't want to go back to France.

"Can't blame you there, mate." He proceeded to cite grievances that dated from Joan of Arc, and in this polite narrative I can't repeat what he called the Maid of Orleans.

Finally a bus appeared for crates, duffle, dogs, and Donald. We were the last passengers off. It was night. I asked the driver to drop us at the taxis but he couldn't. "Cabs are after immigration control," he explained. "Sorry, you'll have to walk." He would drop my 500s at the cab rank.

By now it was 9 p.m. and my fellow ferry passengers were long departed. I slung the duffle over one shoulder, the carry-on over the other, and trudged through a dimly lit, cavernous immigration hall. Luke and June trotted along like they did this every day of their lives.

We popped around the corner into British officials, having a cuppa, relaxing between ferries. June turned on her charm and I mentioned the World Trials. They'd seen something on the telly. Without asking for papers or passport they passed us through to the taxi rank.

Outside. British air. We'd done it. Luke, June, and I were breathing *British air*.

The second cab in the rank was an SUV — big enough for all my gear, but my choice offended the first cab's driver, to whom I apologized for flaunting taxi protocol. Where was he going to put two 500s? On his roof?

As we disassembled crates, my Pakistani driver opened his cellphone to a screenshot of his Doberman. "Stella is my Everything," he confessed happily.

My blue folder had directions to the B&B, and moments later we were winding through steep, narrow medieval streets beneath Dover Castle.

I thought we were booked into a B&B that accepted dogs. As it turned out I'd booked the B&B's annex: a fourth floor, partly renovated walk-up apartment. Four flights. I was glad to leave the 500s with the proprietor. I was grateful the shower worked.

I fed Luke and June. They slept like they were dead.

"That's a Good Boy"

UNLIKE DOG SHOWS and obedience matches, no autocracy determines who can judge a sheepdog trial. The trial host hires who he wants. Since the judge may be judging his neighbor, the fellow he sold an expensive dog to last week, or even his own spouse, the judge's reputation in the sheepdog community is the only check on all too human frailties.

As it happens the concern for reputation among one's peers ensures fairness at least as well as formal rules. Complaints about dog-show judging are common as dirt. Complaints about sheepdog judging are rarely heard.

David Rees has judged hundreds of trials in Britain and the States. Three years ago he sold his Welsh hill farm and moved to California, a decision he came to regret. David returned to Wales, renovated a Bryn Amman bungalow, and hopes to buy the hill pasture behind the house. He's a friendly man who knows everybody in the sheepdoggy microcosm as well as the character and working habits of thousands of sheepdogs living and dead.

Barbara Carpenter is our mutual friend. Barbara owned the famed sire Brocken Robbie, organized the UK's first ladies' sheepdog trial, and wrote definitive histories of sheepdog champions (*The Blue Riband of the Heather* and *National Sheepdog Champions*). In 1999, the ISDS awarded Barbara its coveted Wilkinson Sword Trophy for lifelong service to sheepdogs. When David and I met at trials, we always exchanged news of the grand old lady.

When I wrote Barbara asking if she knew someone who could put Luke and June on Welsh Mountain Sheep — the sheep they'd work at the World Trials — David replied for her, e-mailing that I should ring him up when I got to Wales.

The dogs and I were booked at a hilltop farmhouse B&B north of Carmarthen, forty minutes from the World Trials. Limousin cattle, sheep, and chickens grazed the farm's seventy acres. Gilcrug Farm was bought ten years ago by a retired shop teacher and his wife for their son, Robin, but mad cow disease, two bouts with hoof and mouth, and shrinking agricultural subsidies have damaged British agriculture. Robin farms evenings and weekends.

I'd chosen Gilcrug (pronounced "Gill-Craig") Farm because, apart from being cheap, it was also dog-friendly. But it had been raining for weeks. "We haven't had a summer, really," my hosts told me. When they came back from their first walk, Luke and June were slathered with red mud.

I couldn't bring mud pies into my neat second-floor bedroom, so I set the 500s in an empty horse stall and that's where the dogs slept.

I'D ARRIVED ten days before the World Trials to acclimatize Luke, June, and Donald to climate, topography, creature and plant smells, light and shadows, those local dialects forming a new work gestalt. Welsh Mountain Sheep would be our adversaries/accomplices and we needed to understand their inclinations and fears.

I didn't know another soul in South Wales and David Rees and I were merely acquaintances, so I was relieved when David returned my call.

"We'll meet Monday morning, say eight o'clock, in Abbotsford." David directed me to his favorite breakfast café.

After proper resets, my GPS fired up but couldn't find Abbotsford. No worries; I had David's directions. Maybe British satellites slept late.

It was an hour to downtown *Ammanford*. Dialects.

In David's favorite café I ordered an egg, bacon, sausage, blood pudding, and tomato. (The waitress understood after David translated —"that's tom-*ah*-to, love.")

David was sorry he hadn't been able to put me up (never crossed my mind he might), but he was housing other American handlers and sleeping on the couch himself. He had found sheep for me to work. Last spring David did Wyn Jaffe's night lambing and David had called in the favor. It was no small favor.

Although they walked through them morning and evening, the Mister and Missus never worked Gilcrug's sheep. Brecon Beacon's hills are as grand and barren as the Scottish highlands and Welsh Mountain Sheep grazed beside every deserted single-track road. Did I let the dogs out to give them a go? No. Was I tempted? You bet I was. But how would you like it if a stranger started practicing his sport in your work? These sheep weren't dog toys — they were honest men's livelihood.

Wyn Jaffe? Wyn Jaffe? "Didn't he judge Kingston a couple years back?"

"Oh yes. There was a controversy I believe."

"Controversy" was putting it mildly. I wasn't at Kingston that year but lurid stories spread fast. Rumor: Wyn'd suggested everyone study his judging book before they ran their dog. Wyn said there were far too many women handlers, and, in any case, they were too fat. After Wyn DQed one hard-of-hearing handler who hadn't promptly quit the course, Wyn'd yelled "Hey! You!," which so incensed the handler he'd brandished his crook at the judge, shouting, "I am Mr. Murphy. I am not 'Hey you!'"

And I heard that when Wyn kibitzed as Bev Lambert headed for the post, she snapped, "Don't you fuck with me!"

If true, it was unheard-of. No sheepdogger, not *ever,* disrespects a judge.

To Wyn's credit, handlers thought he got the rankings right (first place went to the best dog, second to the next best, and so on), but Kingston's tempest in a teapot boiled for weeks.

"Mind," David cautioned me, "Wyn does like to get in your face."

THE JAFFE SMALL HOLDING was wonderfully neat. David gestured. "Wyn's kennels are nicer than some people's homes."

Flower beds bordered the front walk and the bungalow was immaculate. The holding offered a spectacular view of the Welsh hills. When I complimented the owner he shrugged. "Oh, the wife cracks the whip on me."

Sans whip, his wife stepped out to promise tea after "Wyn has seen your dogs."

I'd come to acclimatize and train. David and Wyn wanted to get a look at some American dogs.

We crossed the road to a rough forty-acre pasture, cut by deep drains (ditches). June spotted the sheep — some two hundred yearlings — but was convinced she knew better than Donald how to get to them. When June started out wrong, I recalled her. I re-sent her six times before June went out properly. After that initial hiccup, June gathered and brought the flock to the lip of a deep drain. After one ovine iconoclast dared cross, her more timid friends followed in flood. The sheep were heavier than I'd expected and several turned on June, but she bent them to her will. We shed five sheep. Those five were desperate to rejoin their mates but June orbited them around the larger flock. Quiet whistled commands: "Clockwise, more clockwise. Now counter-clockwise! Walk up on the sheep! Clockwise again!" It was a fine exercise, testing June's balance, her willingness to come off balance when asked, her ability to outface resistant sheep — not to mention testing Donald's sheep/sheepdog reading skills and timing.

Luke's outrun was impeccable and — to my delight — he downed at my whistled "Stop!" I kept him damped down on the fetch. The sheep moved off Luke more readily than they had for June. I repeated the orbiting exercise. After a few minutes, one ewe broke, dashing to rejoin the main flock. Luke won't tolerate insubordination, but before he took her down I yelled, "Get out of that!" and called Luke back to me.

Two lifetime dog men had been evaluating the Mister and Missus and when I rejoined them I defused a potentially awkward moment. "Luke's the better," I said.

"Aye," Wyn sighed. "I was just saying so to David."

David asked about Luke's breeding and had he any pups on the ground? I said Luke and June had had one litter.

I swapped my muddy wellies for sandals before following David and Wyn into the Jaffes' parlor, a cozy warm room attached to a sunroom with a stunning view of the mountains.

At table, Wyn told me he'd written a book on judging but had been disappointed in the result. "Not one letter in *Working Sheepdog News*." He grinned. "I'm thinking I'll write one myself."

He said he wanted to encourage controversy and gave me two copies of his small green pamphlet. Later when I read it I thought, yes, it would have encouraged controversy.

Wyn's wife asked how I liked my tea?

"Milk, please."

"No sugar?"

"No, thank you."

"Good boy."

Sugarless David was also a "good boy."

"It will take an awful lot of sugar to sweeten Wyn," David said.

Wyn grinned, gratified.

We gossiped: dogs, family, last night's telly.

Wyn's wife said, "Early on, when I began seeing Wyn, I was having supper with his family when Wyn asked his sister to put his sugar in his tea for him."

"I must have looked at Wyn strangely because he asked me, 'How should I know how much sugar I take?'"

"It Can't Have Been
Easy to Arrange"

THE NEXT DAY David Rees and I drove to David Streeter's steading. Streeter is a landscaper and, David Rees told me, "a demon
for work." Although Streeter rarely took a day off, today was his
birthday and his wife had insisted.

The Streeters' steading was protected by two perfectly hung iron gates.
It had rained more during the night; the fields were soggy and Streeter's
quarter-acre pond was toffee colored. The bungalow was bigger than most
single-family Welsh homes. Streeter had built it himself, one room at a
time, as he could afford materials. He'd not borrowed a penny.

We left our wellies in the unfinished master bedroom — the newest
addition, presently a storeroom.

In his late forties, David Streeter has a familiar Welsh build: he's shaped
like a .38 cartridge and has the latent energy of one. His wife, Coleen, is
lovely.

Straightaway the three men went out to work dogs.

June was workmanlike but sliced her flanks (buzzing the sheep and
alarming them). After Luke ran, David Rees shook his head: "I like him
better every time I see him. I can't understand why nobody's bred to him."

David Streeter asked, "Will you want to work your dogs again after
lunch?"

"Sure."

"Then we won't hose them down. I'll just pop them in a kennel."

Breeding, starting, and selling dogs was David Streeter's second income
and trial handlers came to him for started dogs. Presently he had an eight-
week-old litter, another just born, and several pups and young dogs, most
already sold. David Rees inspected each dog and picked up every newborn.

Coleen Streeter asked her husband to not let the pups out until he'd locked up her chickens.

I smiled. "Come on, an eight-week-old pup can't hurt a grown hen."

"Five pounds on it?" David Streeter stuck out his hand.

I chickened out of the wager and David turned the new litter out to zoom and tumble. David Rees put a pup inside the chicken yard. Eight weeks old, it dropped its silly tail, crouched, and gathered the flapping, outraged hens. Another puppy wasn't interested, a third pup dove in. One pup stayed outside the yard watching every move. I rather fancied that one.

David brought a two-year-old gyp into his training yard. She was quick, keen, and responsive. David told us the gyp preferred sheepwork to people. The tricolor dog he tried next was calmer and quieter around the sheep. He was the dog, David Streeter said, that Welsh trial handlers prefer.

Me, I liked the hotter, people-indifferent gyp. American trial dogs are pushed hard. Train, train, train, not enough (relaxing) practical work, then twelve hours in the car, brand new environment, unfamiliar sheep, and the intense focus of the trial, before twelve hours home for still more training.

Real work is the best teacher for man and dog. Hill lambing teaches the dog that if he doesn't work properly, he'll wear himself out before the day is done. Proper stockwork is economical and precise for the shepherd, the dog, and the sheep.

A few years back, I rode along with four sheepdogs trailing (not "trialing") three thousand ewes seventy miles over Montana's ten-thousand-foot Gravelly Mountains. At the end of the trail at the home ranch those dogs were fresher than dogs after twenty minutes running a sheepdog trial.

At noon we went in to wash up and while we were waiting for the dinner bell, David Streeter brought out a sheaf of pedigrees. I recognized a Scottish dog I saw in 1988 and the Davids asked about him.

"Taff won the Grampian series but gripped off at the International," I recalled.

Dogs long gone. Dogs remembered. How about the dog John Thomas bought for a penny.

He'd had this terrible wreck, you see. Sheep everywhere. Furious owner.

"I can't just take the dog. I have to give you something for him."

"Give me a penny, then. That's all the damn beast is worth!"

The dog went on to place at the International.

And there was the old South Wales shepherd who'd never run a national trial in his life. The sheep were fresh off the hill, shy as virgins, and nobody'd been able to get a shed. The old boy brought the sheep into the shedding ring and paused to take out his pipe, pack it, fire it up, and take a few puffs. This ordinary, unexciting procedure settled the sheep, who dropped their heads and began grazing. The old herd tucked his pipe away, walked into the ring, shed two, won the trial, and never ran a national trial again.

I'd eaten a full British breakfast at 7:30 and now had a second. Table talk was about family and David's birthday party, which would be a joint celebration: David and his daughter had been born on the same day. "Clever that," David Rees observed. "It can't have been easy to arrange."

That afternoon, David Rees and I drove around the Wales he'd grown up in. His father had been a coal miner but at considerable sacrifice sent his daughter to university and David to trade school. David shook his head. "When my sister asked for a horse — a *horse* — somehow he found the brass."

His father had been heartsick when David took up shepherding, but in his later years the old miner would sit on the front step of David's hill farmhouse and survey the green world at his feet, "like he was Lord of the Manor."

These days, David wanted pasture for a few sheep but didn't intend to farm again. "When you get older," he said, "you want to walk to the pub."

This excellent day was spoiled when, after dropping David home, I wrecked my car.

Welsh Roads
(A Rant)

Of course our roads are small. Wales is a small country.

FOR A THOUSAND YEARS men battled over Welsh soil. Fertilized by men's blood, every inch of it is precious, and very, very little is devoted to roads. Driving home one evening outside Nantgaredig, my headlights picked up a woman rolling a stroller on the shoulder, which was all of two feet wide. Her husband preceded her and the family's Border Collie preceded him. I swung wide around this suicidal procession.

Welsh village sidewalks are so narrow, lovers walk in single file. On some, Romeo and Juliet sidle along sideways.

British "M" roads are like US interstates interrupted by occasional roundabouts artfully designed to terrify tourists. M roads are driveable and Welsh two-lane roads aren't bad. The one-and-a-half-lane roads are the knuckle-whiteners. The single tracks are wide enough for bicycles and walled with impenetrable eight- and ten-foot hedgerows so you can't see around the next bend. Since these lanes skirt ancient boundaries they proceed straight for a hectare or so before making a ninety-degree turn at somebody's barn. When one meets an oncoming car/tractor/milk truck, each driver tries to recall where the nearest turnout may be.

Road signs are in Welsh and English. I became rather fond of the Welsh "araf," which means "slow," so the string of cars behind the slowpoke Yank could shaddup and quit with the honking already!

In villages, cars park half on the sidewalk, half in the street, and prudent parkers fold their outside mirrors. At the village newsagents and takeaways, customers park half on the sidewalk.

The first driver into a narrowing has the right to proceed in the wrong lane until he discovers a gap between parked cars big enough to tuck into so the oncoming driver can slip by. Clicked mirrors are the Welsh "How-de-do!"

All this would've been bearable if my car wasn't bass-ackwards. I got in on the wrong side, fumbled with controls with my left hand, told Luke to lie down ("Damn it! I can't see through you!"), and adjusted my mirrors, wrong (right) mirror first. If it had rained during the night (surprise!) I rolled my right (wrong) window down to wipe the mirror.

And away we go!

For me, speed limits were an aspiration; for the Welsh, they're hated reminders of three hundred years of the English telling them what to do. The speed cameras provide Welsh drivers with 90 mph portraits to place with other prized memorabilia on their mantelpieces. Although I admired Welsh savoir-faire I burned more adrenalin than gasoline.

I suppose it's sound policy to give natives an advantage over visitors: live locally, drive maniacally.

Get a grip, Donald! Small women and pensioners drive these roads every day!

After a lovely day with David Rees, I turned toward home during what passed for Ammanford's rush hour. A lorry loomed too close too fast and I misjudged and clipped a parked car's mirror. Instantly, I was as unhinged as that clipped mirror and my hands jerked the car LEFT for safety, exactly as I would have at home. I dynamited my brakes but smacked a parked car, bounced over the curb, and jerked to a stop five feet from a telephone pole. Luke had slid onto the floorboards. June bounced off the back of the front seat. My air bags hadn't deployed. My hands shook as a woman tapped at my window: "Are you all right?"

I got out and walked back to inspect the damage: her car's street-side fenders were destroyed. I said we should call the police. She said I needed a cup of tea.

Glenda Nottingham was more concerned about me than her car. Since nobody had been hurt, the Welsh police (Heddlu De Cymru) weren't interested. The rental people asked if the car was driveable. I tried. Nope. I probably broke an axle when I hit the curb. I phoned David but he wasn't home.

Directly, the Nottingham family gathered: Glenda's husband, her son,

Silas, Silas's wife, and Glenda's grandson. The man whose mirror I'd broken spoke to the rental people too.

My hands wouldn't stop shaking. Glenda insisted I drink a second cup of tea.

Escaping their kindness, I went outside to wait for the removal van (wrecker). It was getting dark. I walked Luke and June. Villagers stopped to ask about my car. They'd seen World Trials promos on the telly. They admired the dogs, who put on a brave show.

I hadn't purchased the optional rental car insurance, believing that since I'd booked on my Amex card, Amex would pay for any damage. I surely hoped they would. My rental Mercedes 150 hadn't been much of a car but it was less car now than it had been.

When Silas offered to drive me to my B&B, I accepted gratefully. As the removal van trundled off with my car, my dog bowls, and my driving glasses, the Mister and Missus lay quietly at my feet.

Oops. Too many singers had shown up for Silas's choir practice so he couldn't drive me home. His elderly parents volunteered. The dogs just fit behind the back seat if they didn't wiggle or take a deep breath.

From Ammanford to Gilcrug Farm took an hour. One way.

Mr. Nottingham broke the ice. He said they'd just returned from Turkey.

"A tour?"

"Oh, no, no. We like to go wherever we want every morning."

Glenda had just the one child, Silas. Her husband had three from a previous marriage. The Nottingham family had once been powerful and rich but had produced too many daughters. Hundreds of Nottinghams attended family reunions.

Asked, I said, "Yes, I have a son. He's 43. Jon's autistic and profoundly retarded. He lives in a group home. I see him twice a year."

"That's terrible."

"Yes."

Mr. Nottingham was internet-savvy. He used it to find guitar-making supplies.

"You're a luthier?"

"Oh, aye."

When I mentioned Martin guitars, he said Martins weren't a spot on his.

The Welsh old folk drove me and my dogs up the moonlit single-track into Gilcrug's farmyard. I said, "How much do I owe for the taxi service?"

"Nought," he said.

"Can I at least pay for your petrol?"

He looked to his wife, who shook her head. "No thanks."

Next morning Glenda Nottingham phoned Gilcrug to ask how I was doing. She called again the day after.

Hafod Bridge

L IKE OTHER foreign handlers who'd compete at the World Trials, I
was desperate to trial on Welsh Mountain Sheep. If practice
was necessary, trials were more so. At a sheepdog trial one's every
unexamined presumption, lazy understanding, or ego-gratifying misreading of dog and/or sheep invites swift retribution.

Some local trials were within driving distance and there'd be special
trials for foreign World Trials competitors before the official World Trials
whoop-de-do.

My Gilcrug hosts drove me into town where I picked up a replacement
rental car.

"Do you have a skinnier car?" I asked dismayed.

"The Vauxhall's all we have at the moment."

It was a big car.

Although many traditional British pubs were closing their doors, Wetherspoon's, a franchise, was thriving and had free wi-fi.

Before I left home I'd been a political junkie, studying polls and attending to pundits.

Over here, I hadn't watched TV or read papers. Now, reading the online
New York Times accounts of political shenanigans, it was hard to give a
damn.

Distance had lifted a burden I hadn't known I'd been carrying. Not-
knowing felt wonderful. Those weighty portents, projections, and pundits
were rumors blown away by the rain, Welsh Mountain Sheep, and two very
muddy sheepdogs.

Next morning, I walked the dogs at five thirty and hit the road in my
big Vauxhall by six. Welsh roads improved when I was the only driver on
them. It had poured all night and was supposed to rain all day, so I was
tricked out in rain pants, rain jacket, and wellies. At a Carmarthen petrol

station I bought a cup of wretched coffee from a machine. My GPS got me fairly close and I stopped at the Llanwrda newsagent for directions to Hafod Bridge. The newsagent was plastered with Countryside Alliance posters, urging everyone to "Protect Rural Britain." The Brits do a better job of countryside protection than we Yanks — who don't really believe any countryside needs protection unless it has a time share where we can take the kids on vacation.

Roads shriveled and bridges were one lane. "Caution!" one sign noted. "Oncoming traffic may be in middle of road."

A paper plate nailed to a fencepost announced "Sheepdog Trial" above an arrow pointing right.

The Hafod Bridge trial was in a muddy ten-acre hill pasture. Its amenities included a khaki WWII snack tent and, to my surprise, two portopots. In 1988 when I first visited the UK, loos at trials were plastic tarps stretched between trees.

The entry fee for two dogs, two runs each was six pounds. The national trial is usual in the UK but the Hafod Bridge trial offered an unfamiliar variant: the South Wales trial. Since I'd never run a South Wales, sure, I'd give it a go.

According to David Rees, some Welsh shepherds ran at three South Wales trials every Saturday. "They'll never run a national but they pick up fifty pounds for a day's work. Not bad, yes?"

South Wales outwork is the same as the national. The dog runs out to the sheep and comes around behind without upsetting them (outrun: 20 points; lift: 10 points; fetch: 20 points).

The South Wales variant begins as the sheep approach the handler waiting in one quadrant of a MALTESE CROSS (20 points). The cross-arms of the freestanding cross are narrow chutes through which the sheep must walk single file. Sheep bunch for safety and when pressured they hate single file. As the lead sheep passes up the cross-arm, she'll arrive at the intersection where she may turn rather than continuing straight. If she stalls beyond the intersection, the sheep behind her may turn down one side or the other.

In a well-executed Maltese, the sheep arrive at the south/north chute, enter, and proceed straight through before the dog flanks around left to fetch them to the mouth of the east/west chute, through which they walk, single file as before.

After the Maltese is negotiated, the dog brings the sheep to a freestanding CHUTE (10 points) through which they must pass.

Although the trial secretary and I had trouble understanding one another's dialect, I entered both dogs, and Mr. MacCeeg was set to go with Lukach. I asked to watch a couple runs to learn the ropes, but the handlers were having a devil of a time. The first dog I watched couldn't get his sheep through the Maltese, and the next dog's sheep got through the Maltese (after much circling and handler bellowing) but balked at the chute.

It was raining—sometimes drumming, sometimes misty drizzle—which bothered me less than it bothered the sheep. Prey animals are spooked when they can't hear or see well: "What's that shape over there, Martha?"

Rain handicaps the dog, too: whistles are harder to hear in a downpour.

In for a penny. Since the previous handler had sent left, I sent left too. Luke made a good outrun and when I whistled, Luke STOPPED (huzzah!). Nice lift, some wobbles on the fetch, but through the fetch panels toward me, standing in the southwest quadrant of the Maltese cross.

I was at a disadvantage because I didn't have a crook. On our farm, I use a metal leg crook to catch sheep. On the trial field, my fancy handmade crook extends my authority and adds five feet to my arm. One flick of the crook spells danger to sheep: "Don't. Go. There!"

But my crook wouldn't fit in my duffle and with two dogs, two 500s, and a sheaf of fret documents (remember that tick shot deadline?), I didn't have the oomph to convince SECURITY that, no, my shepherd's crook wasn't meant to beat the airliner crew to death, snatch the controls, and crash into whatever terrorists crash into.

So I didn't bring the damn crook.

Luke delivered three yearlings to the mouth of the south/north Maltese chute and I fluttered my Stetson in their faces. The sheep stopped in their tracks. Probably never saw a Stetson before.

Luke kept the sheep from escaping up his side of the Maltese. Me and my trusty Stetson held our side.

The ground was muddy and slick. Falling, besides bruises, soppy clothes, and the amusement of the Welsh, meant that the sheep would GET PAST ME. Can't have it.

Since I'd never run a South Wales trial I made assumptions. Didn't know — assumed — that so long as our sheep stayed in the mouth of the Maltese Luke and I weren't losing points.

Respect and trust are the currency of mammalian survival. Luke has tremendous moral authority with sheep.

The work turned into an exercise in patience. I'd ask Luke six inches forward and down him. I'd back off when I was putting too much pressure on the sheep. When they thought to slip past me, they encountered an unfamiliar human fluttering — what? A hat?

Patience — tense, desperate patience. We edge the sheep to the chute opening; twelve inches away, now six. The lead sheep's eyes dart here and there, seeking any alternative. On his elbows with his ass in the air, Luke bows to his sheep. He is smiling. He is quivering.

I don't know how much time we've used. I daren't look away at my watch.

Finally, the leader accepts her fate and trots into the chute. I swiftly back off to take pressure off her two pals who (I hope) will follow her. "Down, Luke! Lie down!" (Stay out of this, Luke. Don't help. Puh-Leeze DON'T HELP!)

At the cross-arms' intersection, the leader hesitates and looks left. I lean toward her and she trots forward as I back up so her pals will follow. All three sheep pass through and are trotting up the hill.

"Luke! Come by!" (Go clockwise.)

Luke breaks in hot pursuit but disagrees —"They're escaping, Boss!"— and races after them ON THE WRONG (counterclockwise) side.

Luke caught them and though he was moving very fast, he didn't upset them. When they arrived at the east/west chute, since Luke and I hadn't harassed them at the first chute, they walked right in.

Exiting, they had reservations ("There's something nasty ahead, Martha. See? That shadow behind those trees?"), and they stalled. I asked Luke to put a little pressure on them. "Steady, Luke! STEADY!"

I assumed the correct line was straight from Maltese to chute and jogged backwards so I could guard my side when the sheep reached the chute mouth.

After a few seconds ruminating, they passed through without further ado.

We were finished. I didn't know whether Luke's going the wrong way to catch the sheep was a fatal or minor fault, but as we came off, the trial secretary said, "Well done." I was shaking and smiling at the same time.

I went under the dank moldy tent for a Welsh cake and a surprisingly good cup of coffee. More rain. Yet more rain. I spoke with two Danish handlers and an Italian woman handler. I liked her dog. I liked a Welsh dog—all black with a white snout.

When she ran later that morning, June was lost in space so I retired her.

We were back to Carmarthen by noon. I ordered a steak at Wetherspoon's pub and ate some of it. When I asked for a doggy bag, the barman sniffed, "We don't do takeaway."

I said, "It's for my dogs."

"We don't do takeaway."

I asked for more napkins, wrapped the meat, and stuck it in my jacket pocket.

It was much appreciated by Luke and June.

Fifteen Minutes of Fame

O N BAD DAYS I think I trial sheepdogs to shorten my time in
purgatory. I was thinking such thoughts at 5:30 a.m. while crossing Welsh mountains in the fog. The roads hadn't improved but
at least I couldn't see them. David Rees had advised, "When you get to
Pen-y-bont village, just ask. Everybody knows Glynn Owens."

More fog. More mountains. I missed Anne. I missed my farm. I missed
my own bed.

American handlers envy the Brits for their numerous local trials. Ours
are hours, sometimes days apart. I intended to run at two trials today. After
the Pen-y-bont trial, I'd feed the dogs in the car and eat something myself
before returning to Hafod Bridge for a second go.

Maybe it stresses dogs running two or three times in a single day; on the
other hand, sheepdog trialing might be easier on the dog when trials are
so routine.

Welsh rivers were out of their banks and homes in Builth Wells were
protected by sandbags. Detour signs directed me around the flood. While
most Welsh trials are "enter when you show up," David had warned that
the Pen-y-bont trial was popular, so I should be there by seven. At seven
thirty, I was still lost. I pulled off and waited politely outside remote farm-
houses until their sheepdogs stopped barking.

"Which Glynn Owens?"

"The sheepdog man."

"Oh aye, aye."

At eight thirty when I finally knocked on the Owenses' door the surprised Mrs. Owens told me the trial was Monday, not today.

"It'll be in that field you passed," she said.

"Thank you, Mrs. Owens. See you then." Dialects.

As it happened, that day every Welsh trial except Hafod Bridge had been cancelled because of flooding. It wasn't for the sake of the handlers or the sheepdogs. The Mister, Missus, and I have run in dust storms, hail, ice storms, and whiteouts. The Welsh trials were cancelled because cars couldn't get to them.

I stopped for coffee and a scone. I filled my gas tank. Foggy Mountain wasn't as foggy but the road was no wider.

I couldn't remember where I'd turned for Hafod Bridge — lots of ll's in the town's name? I got trapped in a back alley in an unpronounceable Welsh village where I reversed several thousand miles between closely parked cars and rubbish bins to let a van scrape by. My three rearview mirrors were too few.

Hafod Bridge. What the hell was the village where I'd turned yesterday? Maybe I should go back to my B&B, curl up in a fetal position, and pull a blanket over my head. Donald! Get a grip!

I motored on, hoping to recognize the village I found yesterday morning before it was light enough to see.

Aha! Llanwrda!! How could I have forgotten you?

Hafod Bridge had more cars than yesterday and I left the Vauxhall a good hike from the field. It was muddier, the entrance was four inches underwater, and the only cars were the trial secretary's and the judge's. In the tent, Welsh strangers conversed in Welsh.

When I sloshed to the trial secretary's car, he rolled the window down, stuck his hand out, and said, "Congratulations, Mr. MaCraig."

I said, "Thank you. For what?"

"You won it, man. The South Wales. We've a cup for you," he answered. "And eighteen pounds." He hesitated with the envelope. "You'll no be wanting a check."

"I can't cash it," I said.

"Very well, I'll get cash for you. You'll stay for your trophy? The presentation?"

You bet I would.

Since I hadn't stayed until the trial ended, I hadn't known what the Welsh sheepdoggers knew. Overnight, Luke's win burned up the bush telegraph. "An American has won Hafod Bridge. And he'd never run a South Wales before. And he worked the sheep with his HAT; he hadn't a crook."

WHEN I PUBLISH a book, I play "minor celeb" for a couple weeks and junior reporters interview THE AUTHOR after covering the Women's Club meeting and before the high school football game. I fondly remember a particular phoner with a college radio station. I suppose the young woman interviewer had the assignment handed her seconds before she dialed, because her first desperate question was, "How long have you wanted to be famous?"

Amazing what they'll ask. I replied, "How would you like to be Paris Hilton? Second question: how much would you pay to *not* be Paris Hilton?"

Okay. The plain truth is I write books — historical novels as well as dog stories — because I can't do anything else well and it's too late to start a career in medicine or as a concert pianist. I'll never be a three-star general, rich, nor a Captain of Industry. I'm probably even too old to become a serial killer, which, like lyric poetry, seems to be a young man's game.

But sometimes, rarely, writing is visions:

On December 13, 1862, at Fredericksburg, Virginia, thousands of Federal soldiers assaulted an impregnable position the Confederates named "the slaughter pen." Five thousand Federal soldiers were wounded or killed. The Confederate victors were hungry and shabby, and shoeless men left bloody footprints in the snow.

When night fell the victors roamed the battlefield, plucking clothing and shoes from the dead. Naked corpses were illuminated by the northern lights, flickering waves of purple and green and blue.

The vision of that night, imagining myself removing a dead man's shoes on that gory, beautiful battlefield — that's why I write.

Fortunately, what celebrity writers enjoy is minor and fleeting.

Sheepdog glory — that's different! Although Luke's win at Hafod Bridge was by any measure inconsequential, it was my fifteen minutes of fame and I reveled in it. No matter that Luke had run early in the day. (The sheep got rank in the afternoon.) No matter that we drew good sheep. It didn't even matter that Luke beat the second-place dog by one point and the third-place by two. That's sheepdog trialing. Luke won the damn trial! When you win a trial, conversations get better because better handlers come over for a chin wag. When you win, your inane opinions become "interesting." When you win your (well-deserved) modesty becomes "good sportsmanship."

STILL, WHATEVER ELSE it may be, fifteen minutes of fame isn't eternity. Today, the spotter was having trouble holding the ewes at the top and, sure enough, one of Luke's three was a rogue. Luke fetched them nicely to the mouth of the Maltese but the third time the rogue tried to break, Luke lost patience and gripped.

The Italian woman with the big Border Collie laid down a nice run.

I chose to run the national trial with June. She said she wanted to outrun left, which was okay by me. Very nice outrun, excellent lift, good fetch. The sheep were bucking and bolting and I fluttered my Stetson to turn them onto the drive. Through the drive panels, good turn, good line, the sheep started to drift downhill and I asked June to cover them and she took THE WRONG FLANK. Missed the panels: we're out of the money. I brought them into the shedding ring where, after some flapdoodle, June split and held two ewes.

Instead of a pen, we faced the chute, where the handler grabs the rope attached to the panel before the sheep enter. As June regathered the sheep, my new friend the trial secretary turned on his PA to shout, "Take the rope, man!"

It's absolutely forbidden to offer help to a handler on the course, but everybody just laughed at the mentally challenged American (winner), and June's sheep went through nicely.

ALTHOUGH WE WOULDN'T be in the prize list a second time, I was glad about June's run. She hadn't been running well, but today, she was back to her reliable, unflashy best self. After all (as she reminded me), it was Missus June, not Mister Luke, who got us over here.

The president of the South Wales Sheepdog Society wore a tan tweed suit, white dress shirt, and ISDS tie. His blunt thick fingers and powerful handshake belonged to a farmer who'd worked with his hands every day of his life.

The president's niece snapped a picture of the president, Luke, me, and the trophy for their newsletter.

He said, "In the hundred two years of the Hafod Bridge trial, no American has ever entered it. And now an American has entered and has defeated the Welsh." He frowned, puzzled. "Do you not use crooks? In America, I mean."

Inscribed on the base of Luke's pewter cup is: "Treialon Cwn Defaid, Hafod-y-Bridge."

It's the thought that counts.

The Standard

J UDGES CALL OFF (DQ) handlers for grips, abusing the sheep, dog off course, failure to progress, and inept work. When a trial is overbooked, after the first dozen runs the judge will call handlers off after they've lost an arbitrary number of points. If that "standard" doesn't relieve overbooking, the judge will raise it and call a handler off if he misses one panel. As a last resort, after the judge has seen six good runs, he will call you off the instant you lose so many points you cannot beat or tie the lowest of the six.

At most big trials, that lowest score of the top six will be in the high 90s of 110 points possible. After the judge has deducted 12 points, he'll honk the horn; you call your dog and walk off. Score: zero.

One hundred fifteen foreign competitors had entered the practice trials for the World Trials. The time limit was nine minutes and the running began at 8 a.m. That's a thousand minutes of running, and since South Wales enjoys thirteen hours of daylight at that time of year, the judge invoked the standard. Most handlers scored zero, and despite the strictest standard the practice trials finished in the dark.

As his wife had promised me, Glynn Owens did host a trial at Pen-y-bont, and I arrived early only to be told that today's trial was for Welsh competitors and I must drive to Brecon for the "foreign competitors" trial. I argued, "I compete with Americans all the time. I've come to Wales to compete with the Welsh."

Nope.

Brits are fussy about protocol and once again (fourth time) I traversed Foggy Mountain. At Brecon, the closest parking was a mile from the trial ground, so both dogs accompanied me.

Usually, I leave Luke in the car until his turn. Luke's so dead keen that any dog working *his* sheep offends him. When I'm working his Missus,

Luke views it as Public Adultery. Frustrated and angry, he growls at pass-ersby (bad form at sheepdog trials), and he digs.

At Brecon, in Welsh soil softened by weeks of rain, Luke dug a dandy fox (dog?) hole, slathering himself with dirt. Except for his gleaming eyes Luke was a mud ball. Luke is a blockhead.

June had a good run going until stupid Donald gave her the wrong com-mand. Later, when Luke got the horn, our judge, David Rees, said, "Don-ald, I hated to hit that horn."

I said, "I hated it too."

David said, "I hear you won Hafod Bridge. Come over some night and we'll christen your cup with wine."

Next day, I finally got to run at Pen-y-bont. It was my third attempt, my fifth time crossing Foggy Mountain. Another wretched morning, cold and — yep — raining. The bad weather didn't faze the aged hunchbacked shepherd leaning against Judge John Thomas's car, chatting with him. The ground was slippery and the old shepherd's crook was firmly jammed into the mud.

Retired shepherds attend all the trials. Sheepdog trials are the same work they did when they were young and hale, and though they may never have trialed and no longer keep sheepdogs, they'd owned the trial dogs' ances-tors and kin. Quirks often accompany the skills we deliberately breed for, and an old man's youth can be rekindled by a dog's inherited wry glance, inimitable jaunty walk, or one-dog-in-a-thousand goofy smile.

Shepherds often hire on at sixteen when they leave school. Sheep thrive on marginal land: hills or moors where profitable row crops cannot be grown. The shepherd's "hill," his workplace, may be five hundred or five thousand acres. Alone on remote, uninhabited, fenceless land, accompa-nied and assisted by his sheepdog, the shepherd may tend a thousand ewes, supervising breeding and lambing, curing ailments and injuries, weaning lambs and gathering them for the market. It is physically demanding, so-phisticated work. Catching a terrified yearling ewe, then repositioning and pulling her mispresented unborn lamb, is all in a day's work.

When I first began to know them, I was startled by the stamina of the hill shepherds. When one of these worthies started up the hill, he walked straight up the damn hill, surmounting gorse and lichen, burns and moraine like his legs were fashioned from leftover mountain goat parts while I — twenty years his junior — tacked back and forth on the slope, gasping for air.

These shepherds remembered every sheepdog they'd owned and, it seemed, every sheepdog they'd ever seen. One evening, feet to the fire and wee dram in hand, the aged Geoff Billingham told me how William Telfer worked Queen. Queen was the smooth-coated, prick-eared granddaughter of Old Hemp, the very first sheepdog in the first (1906) ISDS registry.

"Queen? Surely not William Telfer?"

Geoff smiled sadly. "Oh, aye, aye. It was William Telfer all right. Donald, it's been forty generations of dogs, but only three generations of men."

Forty generations of dogs.

I was middle-aged when I bought Pip. Pip's gone now seventeen years. What a grand, hard-headed dog he was. When my instructions baffled him, he'd dance around me and worry my cuffs or nip at my legs.

Who would I have become if I'd depended on dogs like Pip or Luke or June for fifty years?

That sixteen-year-old, alone on the vast, empty hill. Days of fluffy clouds and luminescent skies and harrier hawks riding thermals. Kneeling beside your dog to drink from an unnamed burn. The terrifying storms: lightning like flashbulbs on your retina, panicked sheep, facefuls of rain.

Stark white winters. Your dog's fur clotted with snow.

"Good boy, Pip. That's a good lad."

Your entire arduous, complex, beautiful life: made possible by your dog. No wonder they came to the trials.

Today, at Pen-y-bont, a Dutch handler and I were bitching about the rain. As the hunchbacked shepherd cautiously picked his way off the slippery field, the Dutchman told me, "That old fellow has come to all the trials. He was in the grandstand at Abergele — in the top row, fast asleep. Had his chin on his hands atop his crook. The crook slipped and if someone hadn't grabbed him he would have rolled down the stairs."

June was spectacularly silly and her sheep missed the fetch panels. I walked off without waiting for the judge's horn.

As Luke and I waited at the post, one sheep split from her pals and drifted toward the fetch panels. Once you send your dog you've "accepted" your sheep and I didn't want this bunch. Judge Thomas signaled for fresh sheep and a pickup dog exhausted the miscreants.

Luke made a nice outrun, pretty good lift and fetch, nice turn around the post, wobbly on the drive and crossdrive (but got his panels), and into the shedding ring for the split. Right away, before either he or I were ready, a space opened and I called Luke in. Confused, instead of coming through, Luke regathered the sheep. No horn. We were still in the prize list with three minutes left.

Luke and I maneuvered to try again.

HONK.

I touched my Stetson in acknowledgment and started my sheep off the course. Judge Thomas jumped out of his car crying, "No, no. That wasn't me. Someone else honked their horn."

Nothing to be done about it. Rightly or wrongly I'd left the course. I laughed. "I don't think I was winning anyway."

He smiled. "Will you be seeing Barbara Carpenter while you're over?" he asked.

"I will."

John shook his head. "She's no been very well."

I said I'd heard that.

He repeated, "Sorry about the horn."

That's sheepdogging.

The Dogs' Sabbath

THE NEXT DAY dawned dry and fine. Wales shook itself like a wet dog and became a green and pleasant land.

Enough was enough. Mr. and Mrs. Dog had endured too many high-stress days.

Yeah, I know: they're only dogs. Yep, life is stress. Would you have done as well as they did? They'd been body-rolled (helpless!) by dog-ignorant TSA strangers, before being bundled into the black, noisy hold of an airliner. Twelve hours later, they'd been loaded into an unstable luggage heap and trundled through thousands of humans that didn't sound, look, or smell like any humans they'd previously known. For a couple hours they'd teetered atop slick plastic crates before being abandoned in a wire cage in the bowels of an exhaust-stinking, clatter/bang/rumble ferry. Another strange car, up four weary flights into an unfamiliar lair before sleep overtook them.

Luke and June crossed Britain from Dover to South Wales and whenever they got out of the car to stretch, they stood on narrow grass verges between busy parking lots and a roaring motorway.

Nothing, absolutely nothing was familiar. The humans they met, grass, plants, sheep, smells, and humidity were new. Even their food was unfamiliar British grub.

The dogs had trained hard, up before daybreak and breakfasting in the car. They'd survived a car crash.

They'd worked and trialed difficult sheep on unfamiliar ground. Their morning and evening walks had been by flashlight. They'd been wet so often their fur stank of mildew.

Home-away-from-home? Two plastic crates in a damp stall.

Throughout, they'd been mannerly. At Dulles, in Charles De Gaulle's nasty parking lot, in the ferry terminal, in buses and taxis, while greeting strangers — whatever I asked, Luke and June had answered. They never sulked, complained, or let the unfamiliar rattle them. They said hello to humans who needed hellos and ignored those who didn't. Amongst hundreds of strange dogs, they kept their own counsel.

Tomorrow would be the opening ceremonies of the World Sheepdog Trials. Luke would run Thursday, June on Friday, and if we were very lucky we'd make the semifinals.

The great absence in their lives had been Dog Time: no requirements, no commands, no leashes, just two dogs alive in the world, sniffing their sniffs, investigating what they would, wandering where they wished to.

So this bright day would be the Dogs' Sabbath.

Downtown Carmarthen's castle isn't much of a castle. Citizens pass through its ruins to the municipal car park. But signs on its parapets told me it had guarded the River Towy and that the ocean — Carmarthen Bay and Cefn Sidan, a famous beach I hadn't heard of — were thirty miles downstream. So close as that?

I jumped Luke and June into the car and away we went.

Yes, the Cefn Sidan gateman assured me, dogs are allowed.

"On the beach?"

"The main beach is closed to dogs until October. But dogs are welcome at either end."

"Okay."

Sternly: "Dogs must be under control at all times."

"I think we can manage that."

The parking lot was surrounded by dunes and a faint trail meandered toward the ocean.

Apparently dune sniffs are something special doggily: June and Luke were agog with joy.

They ran here. They ran there. They asked doggy questions of the world while I climbed over one dune and up the next.

On the broad empty sand beach Luke and June rolled and rolled, tongues lolling, being just as silly as they needed to be.

"Why here's some flotsam: how fascinating!"

"A fishing net float! Hey! Bizarro!"

A grinning June suggested to Luke that they might "play," but the old stick-in-the-mud wasn't interested.

The dogs dashed, they rolled, they had a big time.

And like tired children, they slept all the way home.

The Parade of
Flags and Dogs

INEFWR COUNTRY Park is an eight-hundred-acre estate with
a grand manor house and the ruins of Dinefwr Castle looming
over what would be June's qualifying field. I never visited either
building.

I buzzed right past hundreds of Welsh historic sites. Wales is famous for
trout streams, craggy hills, and sublime vistas. I cursed the narrow bridges
over the streams and wished I could work the sheep I spotted on the hills.

Sheepdog trialing fills up the brain. There's only enough room left for
laughter.

When British sheepdoggers come to the States to judge, they get to see:
(1) their host's home, (2) his favorite restaurant, and (3) one tourist attraction if it's not more than thirty minutes from the trial grounds. Their pay?
Expenses. They do see sheepdogs they wouldn't have seen. It's about the
dogs. Always the dogs.

As soon as the World Trials grounds opened, 210 international handlers
traversed every foot of the qualifying courses, trying to guess what this particular topography would mean to the sheep and the dogs working them.

Pre-trial preparation is only somewhat useful — the real thing starts
when the sheep are spotted and Mister or Missus Dog leave my feet — but
I'd feel a fool if I didn't study the course.

In ten runs since we came to Wales Luke and June had each run well five
times and Luke was brilliant once. My handling had been iffy. I'd misread
sheep, miscommanded twice, and generally failed to master the flowing
gestalt of sheep, course, and sheepdog. Excepting Luke at Hafod Bridge,
I hadn't done right by my dogs, and even at Hafod Bridge I should have

anticipated Luke's decision to run up the wrong side of the Maltese. We were lucky my lapse didn't cost us the trophy.

Sometimes pressure narrows my focus and I'm free to take chances I usually don't dare. Usually I need a GPS to find my buttocks with both hands.

At the Llandeilo Rugby Club's makeshift RV camp, the Italian woman I'd met at Hafod Bridge told me her camper was full of water and offered me a glass of grappa. Upstairs in the club I collected my goody bag with official vests, car passes, badges, program, rule books, gimmee cap, and other tchotchkes too numerous to mention. We Americans sat at a long table swapping adventure yarns and devouring Welsh cakes.

In the late afternoon, we migrated into the tiny village's central car park: two hundred handlers, half again that many dogs, and Llandeilo's rush-hour commuters trying to start home without running over a sheepdog.

For a surprise, it started to rain.

After we milled around the car park for an hour, trial officials sent us down Prince Street, a twenty-foot thoroughfare with cars squeezing through in both directions while spectators overflowed the narrow sidewalks. "Oh, what a handsome Collie. Can I pet him?"

It rained harder.

Some spectators had been waiting here for hours. Not much excitement in Llandeilo, I guess.

With excuses in many languages, we handlers eased our dogs along.

Mustered into a cobblestoned square, we formed national teams. We Yanks wore bright red World Team jackets. (Team Germany had the coolest team jackets, though Sweden's were a close second.)

It rained harder.

Television cameras eyed us glassily. Sound men got tangled in dog leashes. Cameramen lay belly-flat on wet cobbles for close-ups of drenched Collies licking their fur.

At long last, the drum major bellowed and the bass drum thumped and we were, in a rag-tag and intensely doggy fashion, parading.

We marched alphabetically — Austria, Australia, then Fiona Robertson, Canada's sole representative, carrying her maple leaf flag. The United

THE PARADE OF FLAGS AND DOGS

States and Welsh teams brought up the rear. Clots of handlers and sheepdogs proceeded down Prince Street as spectators cheered and applauded
each national team.

More television, more cameras. More rain.

Llandeilo is no metropolis, but I swear there were five thousand people
on balconies or spilling off the sidewalks into the street, cheering louder
than the drumming rain. Our team captain, Alasdair MacRae, waved the
American flag. Alasdair had removed his rain slicker in honor of the occasion and his nice blue blazer was soaked black.

Schoolchildren had made paper flags which fluttered enthusiastically
when each child's chosen team paraded past. Boy Scouts saluted. Ambu-
lance corpsmen in bright lime-green uniforms gave us a cheer.

The United States team drew applause, but the Welsh exploded when
their flag appeared.

ROOAAR!!!!

June flinched. Luke hated every second of it. Although this whoop-up
was in the sheepdogs' honor I can't imagine one of them enjoyed it.

Dogs will tolerate almost anything to be with us.

Bad Sheep

ASCOT MUTTERED, "I've been coming to Wales for sixty years and I've never seen so much rain."

Every Welsh man and woman I'd met at the smaller trials was working the World Trials today. There were food kiosks (my favorite: "Mobile Indian Cuisine"), a Renault exhibit, crook makers, a cider and perry maker, and an outdoors clothing tent Carhart might have envied. One could buy Australian boots or Border Collie figurines, and the big crowds wouldn't be here until the weekend. Land Rover was the lead sponsor and probably you could have bought one of their cars, but it wouldn't have done you much good. The stoutest 4WDs couldn't move in this mud.

I admired Welsh unflappability. Since cars couldn't drive in or out of the designated car parks, buses ferried spectators from Llandielo. Since we handlers had our dogs with us, we were allowed in before the turf was broken. Thirty feet of rubber matting protected the entryway until it sank beneath dark red mud. We crept onto the qualifying fields past two giant 4WD tractors. Their cheerful drivers were drinking coffee. Seven-thirty a.m., raining.

Dogs would run simultaneously on three different qualifying courses. From each course, the top fourteen competitors would get through to the semifinals. Although I had no realistic hope of reaching the Sunday finals (the dreaded/much-desired double lift), if Luke or June were in top form, if we drew good sheep, if we had luck and I didn't screw up, we could get through to the semifinals.

That was as far as my vision could carry me. I'd hoped we could qualify for our National Finals. I'd dreamed we could win through to the United States Team. Now, I prayed we could get through the World Trials qualifying.

I wanted more than a second fifteen minutes of fame.

Imagine yourself walking onto a beautiful green pasture, conversing with the dog at your side. A joke? Was that one of Luke's blockhead jokes? Just another day of the work you both know and love to do.

There ahead: five sheep. Lovely beasts; see how the sun glistens their wool.

And your dog is away, confident and keen, wondering what this job would demand. Your whistle's ready but you won't need it. The dog kicks in behind the sheep and announces himself. "Good morning, ladies. Just a few things I'll ask you to do."

"Why of course, dear. Emily! Fall in! Don't dawdle."

You ask your dog for subtle adjustments but his flocklet trusts him and he keep things settled. You react to every sheep intention before they know *what* they intend. When they come into the shedding ring, your dog shoots you a glance, asking, "Which?" You tell him and he does it. No fighting, no muddle, nothing but dog/sheep/you disappeared in the universe of the moment.

No, it doesn't happen often but it *does* happen.

Visions. Today might be a day for them.

BY UNHAPPY COINCIDENCE, I'd been profiled in the latest issue of *Working Sheepdog News,* the bible of the sheepdog world. While I'd been appropriately modest about my sheepdog skills I was, willy-nilly, a media star: a cover-Yank.

Working Sheepdog News and Luke's unlikely win at Hafod Bridge had put a spotlight on a not-ready-for-prime-time handler.

"McCaig? Say, aren't you the fellow . . ."

My bright plastic vest said "214" in big numbers. Luke and I would be the fourteenth team on qualifying field two. In my clumsy head-to-toe raingear, I couldn't tie my vest properly, so a retired shepherd helped me. I did have a crook today. My Gilcrug landlady had loaned me her cane.

Rain-garbed handlers and retired shepherds sat in cars or leaned on them gossiping. No sensible spectators had come out in this muck.

Each run would be judged by judges from two different countries. A perfect score would be 220. To advance to the semis, you'd probably want 175 or better.

Five Welsh Mountain ewes. Three days ago they had been plucked from their remote, satisfactorily boring grazing—"Sorry for yawning, Martha, hear anything new this month?"—and suddenly dropped into sheep hell. STRANGE DOGS! UNKNOWN PEOPLE! NOISE! "Martha! Is this the end!?"

Consequently, these sheep were skittish as spit on a hot griddle. Of the first thirteen runs, only one dog was able to settle them and not one dog penned. Since the spotters couldn't hold the sheep until the competing dog got behind and took control, a third spotter and dog had been sent down the course to wait in front of the fetch panels and discourage sheep from bolting toward them the moment they saw a dog five hundred yards away.

It was the kind of course Luke favored. Sheep never out of sight during the short downhill and longer upslope outrun. Wide enough sent right, narrow on the left. He'd fetch them downhill through fetch panels, through a dip, then uphill to my feet. At this trial, wooden stairs were the handler's post. Atop, I'd be able to see Luke and his sheep in that dip.

Around the stairs then drive the sheep three hundred yards downhill and traverse the hill four hundred yards on the crossdrive.

After Luke returned the sheep up slope into the shedding ring, we'd shed two of the three uncollared sheep before proceeding to the pen, which these sheep disliked a lot.

At the 2003 Finals in Sturgis, South Dakota, the sheep were so man-shy one tiny flick of your crook would frighten them over the dog. At Sturgis, of seventy dogs, only two penned. These Welsh Mountain Sheep weren't quite as bad, but the dog had to do most of the work without much help from the handler. Splitting two unmarked ewes was difficult; singling one collared ewe after the pen was less so (provided, of course, that Luke and I got that far).

The judges were sequestered atop a tower behind the course. The announcer named each handler, his dog, and their country of origin. He asked me if he could say, "Donald is from Williamsville, Virginia, in the

States. Williamsville has a population of sixteen, now fifteen since Donald's in Wales."

Sure. What the hey?

I sat on the hood watching while Luke snoozed in the car.

I pretend a calm I don't feel. Soothing nonsense in a cracked voice, slow movements to conceal my trembling hands.

Do I fool Luke? Probably not. But my effort may reassure him: "If Donald's as goofy as he usually is, at least he's no worse."

"Number two-fourteen, Donald McCaig with Luke. Donald comes to us from Williamsville, Virginia . . ."

Luke shivered with desire as his sheep came onto the field. I began walking toward the stairs/handler's post but before we were there, without my command, Luke started outrunning. So I pretended I'd sent him and clicked my timer. "That's right, Mr. Judges. We Americans always send our dogs without apparent cue." Fifteen minutes counting down.

I anticipated trouble at the pen. These skittish sheep wouldn't like pushy, powerful Luke and when he urged them to enter a pen (SHEEP TRAP! SHEEP DANGEROUS!) they wouldn't wanna.

I got trouble sooner than I'd anticipated.

Luke was a shade tight on his outrun so I blew him out. Luke widened, but fifteen seconds before he might have arrived behind his sheep they bolted, overran the fetch panel spotter and his dog, and were at the fetch panels. I asked Luke to kick in the afterburners and catch the runaways before they passed the fetch panels. He caught them one second after.

Though the sheep never slowed from a dead run, Luke put them back on the fetch line as they raced uphill toward my stairs/post. Five flying sheep surmounted the hill to confront several hundred spectators. "Martha, I'm having palpitations!"

"Save your breath, honey. Run!"

They wanted to come around wrong way but I blocked them and Luke brought them properly.

But they never slowed down. Luke wasn't controlling these sheep, he was pursuing them. Controlling sheep is what a sheepdog does. Controlling sheep is Luke's raison d'être.

As they hurtled downslope toward the drive panels, Luke raced around them and turned into their faces. The sheep stopped. Finally. Dead stop.

Luke's desperate move wasn't silly or impractical. He'd regained control. But heading sheep on the drive is a grievous fault and the judges' pencils would be busy.

Briefly Luke established a decent pace on the crossdrive, but the sheep bolted again and Luke was so far behind, he couldn't catch and turn them through the crossdrive panels.

We were toast. No hope of qualifying; we'd lost far too many points. But I did want to try the uncollared split for experience. Alas, when the sheep topped the hill a second time, Luke wasn't listening to me.

I couldn't blame the sheep. The lead ewe was high-headed — she'd been jerked from her familiar world into the radically unfamiliar and she wanted no part of it. "Martha, give me half a chance and we're away!"

I couldn't blame Luke either. His eyes were blazing. He had had it with that lead sheep. If I persisted and attempted the split, that lead ewe was going to bolt again and this time, Luke was going to take her down. Satisfying for Luke, and maybe she deserved it. But sheepdog trialing is about livestock, not justice, and if I pressed on our ugly run was going to get uglier.

So I tipped my hat to the judges, said, "Luke that'll do. Luke, that'll DO!," and my dog and I walked off. The courteous applause was for knowing when to quit.

Luke was pissed. I was dazed.

I'm a pretty good mud driver but the Vauxhall sank to the axles. With great good humor, a tractor crew located a towing eye in my car's tool bag, pried open a hatch on the front fender, screwed in the eye, hooked to it, and pulled me and my dogs to asphalt.

Absently I thanked my rescuers.

I couldn't take my mind off our wreck. Ordinarily, I send Luke quietly: "Just another day's work, Lukey." If I'm muttering as we walk to the post, Luke never starts on his own.

Sheep easily read dogs five hundred yards away. Did his self-start scare them? He was only slightly tight, did it unnerve them further? They bolted while Luke was running properly wide two hundred fifty yards from them. Why did they bolt downhill, toward Luke, instead of away to the side?

Perhaps the sheep spotter couldn't hold them and let them go too early.

Sometimes reflection passes time pleasantly; sometimes it stretches time like taffy.

There's a Scottish sheepdogger's joke:

Little Sheila's in bed when her father returns home, very late Sunday night. He slams the car door. He jerks the kennel door open and snarls, "Get in there!" He bangs the kennel shut.

Sheila goes to her window and in a tremulous voice asks, "Bad sheep again, eh, Da?"

Eternity in an Hour

L UKE WAS OUT OF the running. June would decide if we got through to the semifinals. How many miles had it been? How many trials on how many fields? How many training sessions? The Latin root of "hallucination" is "alucinatus": "to dream."

I can't watch *Antiques Roadshow* or the Super Bowl without marveling at our ability to care about zip-shit. Two million dollars for a pasteboard baseball card? A $27 million annual paycheck for a person uncommonly skilled at hurling a fourteen-ounce football? Our visions are more important than CAT scans. All we featherless bipeds yearn to hold eternity in an hour.

Luke, my sometime miracle worker, was kaput.

June is plain vanilla. When I bought the fourteen-month-old smooth-coated gyp she didn't like to walk into sheep facing her, but she was clever. If she ran at sheep full tilt and "bumped them," instead of facing her in a rude threatening manner, the sheep panicked and ran.

"Well," June patiently excused herself, "as you may have noticed: the sheep are MOVING."

And so they were. Flat out, their mindfulness in tatters and their flocking glue unstuck. With a wolf on their heels, sheep hit the panic button.

Unthinking sheep cannot be controlled. On the trial field they often separate, two and three or (worse) one and four. A single sheep facing a sheepdog/wolf is reduced to one instinctual urge: ESCAPE. Over dog, over fence —"Martha, there'll be time to think LATER!"

But June is clever and she eventually learned that sheep facing her, lowering their butting heads, and pawing the earth were almost always bluffing and if they weren't she could dodge their charge. She also learned that when sheep panicked she had to run wider and miles further to reassert control.

June doesn't like to work harder than needs be, and, like most sheepdogs, she has a highly developed aesthetic sensibility. Bumping sheep created, er, *tacky* results.

But June never entirely forgot that handy little trick. While she no longer "bumps" sometimes she "buzzes" them: June likes to make sheep jump. When they are resolutely uncooperative or dullards, June disciplines them by coming so close their ovine blood pressure skyrockets, their minds go blank, and they LEAP. That's June's sheep buzz. It makes her feel like a puppy again. June knows she oughtn't but sometimes they push her too far. If my whistles get excited, June takes my panic as permission.

Judges do not approve of the sheepdog buzzing the sheep. They deduct points — sometimes many points — for that fault. If they think the sheepdog was attempting a grip they may disqualify the dog and it's no good explaining June never BITES sheep she just likes to BUZZ them.

"Sir. Thank you very much." (Sheepdog trials are the only sport I know where you're disqualified with deliberate courtesy.)

Excepting her one character flaw, June is a dependable worker. She's a good listener and rarely loses her temper.

In any case it was too late to break her of the habit. It was too late to introduce her to five or ten more venues or sheep breeds she hadn't worked before. Tomorrow afternoon, number 362, sixty-second dog to run on qualifying field three. Showtime.

When reality fails, visions intercede. June's life coach, Rachael, was enrolled in film school at the University of Texas. Let's see: that'd be central daylight time, six hours earlier. Rachael'd be up by now.

"Hi Rach . . . Oh, not too bad . . . Raining. I never saw so much rain. Doing okay. Luke won a trial . . . June runs tomorrow, probably about two o'clock. Say, can I ask a favor?"

In my Gilcrug bedroom, June lay quietly with her chin on her paws.

"Thanks, Rach."

I held my cellphone to June's doggy ear so Rachael could whisper advice, prayers, and magic incantations. I'm not proud.

FRIDAY MORNING was dry. The sun was out and for the first time in days I left my moldy rain gear in the car. I'd almost left Luke in his Gilcrug crate but he'd been crated ten hours overnight, and popping him back for ten more after a thirty-minute predawn walk seemed cruel.

Yesterday, scores of 190 (of 220) got through to the semifinals. June and I couldn't lose more than fifteen points per judge. A high hurdle. At many American trials fifteen off would take first place. You may recall June's qualifying run at our Nationals was 127.

She would run on field three, the trial's remotest field, under the broken parapets of Dinefwr castle. Field three was a steep bowl rising from the handler's post for a five-hundred-yard outrun. Sending left would give June more room and the slope was less likely to pull her in tight.

These Welsh Mountain Sheep had been run once yesterday on this field, and the sheep who'd been successfully penned were less frightened of it. Those who'd evaded the pen had learned new tricks.

If the outrun and lift were correct, the sheep came off nicely. June couldn't push them, I'd want her well behind.

The first hazard was the crossdrive. After they got through the drive panels, the sheep turned down a steep bank which started them running. Five speeding Welsh Mountain Sheep are unsteerable. Handler after handler missed the crossdrive panel, usually low.

The next hazard was the split — handlers came to grief separating two (of the three) uncollared sheep from the two collared ones. Handler on one side of the miniflock, dog on the other, and oft as not a collared sheep standing at either end.

Unlike Luke, June is an uninspired shedder.

The loudspeaker crackled as scores were announced: the better runs today were in the high 190s. To get through, June and I needed the best run of our lives.

As technical rock climbers say, "Having fun doesn't mean you have to have *fun*."

I was surprised how many British sheepdoggers I knew. I'd met their dogs on previous visits, they'd judged me at American trials. We were all part of one odd doggy community.

Some had read my books, most hadn't. My *Eminent Dogs, Dangerous Men* had created a tempest in a teapot. A couple years ago, at a Scottish trial, a young man shook my hand: "Oh aye. You're the one wrote the book." *The* book indeed.

Thomas Longton, a brilliant handler from a famous sheepdog family, introduced me to a shepherd. "This is Donald McCaig. He's a famous author."

The shepherd eyed me for other deviance. "Oh, aye. Aye."

It was too hot to leave Luke in the car and I hadn't a tie-chain, so I found a shady spot and tied him to a fence.

An American teammate said I'd need a new health certificate to fly my dogs home.

"A health certificate? Where do I get a health certificate?"

Shrug. "There's a vet in Llandielo."

Standing beside the judges' tower, Thomas Longton and I critiqued the runs. It's easier to be right on the spectators' side of the fence. Stepping through the gate onto a trial field is like stepping into a thick, chilly mental fog.

"MS. FIONA ROBERTSON from Quebec, Canada, will be our next competitor. Will Donald McCaig from Williamsville, Virginia, please stand by?"

I went to check on Luke, who was tangled in his string lead and had dug himself a foxhole. I had a second string lead but was afraid to double-tie him for fear he'd choke himself to death. I admonished him sternly.

FIONA'S DOG STALLED between the crossdrive panel and the shedding ring. The sheep had got the moral upper hand and the poor dog couldn't shift them. I'd bet Fiona would have welcomed a buzz.

Okay. Take a deep breath. Step through the gate.

At the post, June and I conversed. She didn't care whether I sent her right or left. Yes, she'd seen the sheep. No seismograph trucks on this field, ha ha.

June was cocked. Hair trigger. Trembling. For better or for worse this seven-year-old sheepdog and I were in this together. "Come by," I whispered to her.

Rachael's invocation took effect: June was in her good-outrun mode, not a thing wrong with it. I whistled her down when she got behind her sheep.

Bright sunlight blessed the emerald pasture beneath the broken castle. June's sheep came out of shade toward the fetch panels. I downed June. I downed her again. Again. And again. These sheep preferred to be worked at a brisk walk.

Five Welsh Mountain Sheep came straight toward the fetch panels, a little quicker than I liked but if I downed June they veered off line, so I kept my dog on her feet.

The lead ewe had a mind of her own; she remembered where the exhaust was and meant to flee there and be done with this trial nonsense. At the handler's post, I brought June around in stages: "Come by/Down!," "Come by/Down!," "Come by/Down!" The turn wasn't tight as I would have liked (2 points off per judge), but it was good enough. Approaching the drive panels we had a bobble (1 point per judge), but at the panels I downed June, held my breath (ARE THE SHEEP THROUGH? ARE THEY? YES!), and flanked June. Nothing wrong with the turn. The sheep picked up their pace.

Three dark green rushes marked the crossdrive line. June's sheep were briefly a hair high (1 point per judge), but back on line as they passed above the fetch panels.

They broke into a run! HANDLER ERROR: At twenty previous runs, if the sheep started running here, they kept running even if you downed the dog: AND I DOWNED JUNE.

Which gave the sheep a big lead, almost-at-the-crossdrive-panels-and-going-to-miss-them until I recovered and whistled JUNE TO THE LAST-SECOND RESCUE.

June's always been quick but even as a young dog she'd never been quicker. Magic. She caught the ewes just below the crossdrive panels when I thought they'd already missed.

When sheep are turned abruptly below panels (2 points per judge for off line — else why would the dog need to turn them?), those sheep almost always lunge uphill and miss the panels on the high side.

But the instant June turned them, in that nanosecond, I flanked June uphill so she caught them and turned them through the opening.

Our run had been imperfect but we hadn't lost enough points to knock us out of the semifinals. We still had 8 or 10 points to play with.

June's crossdrive turn was too wide — 1 or 2 points per judge.

As our sheep approached the shedding ring, I checked my watch: eleven minutes for the split, pen, and single. Eleven minutes is June's and my fair portion of eternity.

June and I let the ewes settle in the shedding ring. "Nothing going on, sheepies. Doo-dah doo-dah . . . Why not have a bite to eat?"

Sheep hate being singled out. Walking softly, I used my cane/crook to shift one collared ewe to the back of the flocklet and an uncollared ewe to the front. In back I'VE GOT MY TWO! But a collared sheep rejoined the two uncollared ewes and queered our chance.

Since I didn't attempt the shed it was a minor fault: 1 or 2 points per judge? The sheep were swirling. Mentally I'd not recovered from our missed opportunity when two uncollared sheep stepped placidly to one end of the flocklet, and by God they were willing to split. I called June in and she marched them briskly away.

June regathered all five and held her recombined flock off the pen until I got there and jerked the gate open.

As the sheep tiptoed (tiphoofed?) warily toward the mouth of the pen, with eons of time and, to this moment, a qualifying score, I lost it. Somehow, and to this day I cannot think why, I forgot that lead ewe with the wandering eye.

I knew these Welsh Mountain Sheep were mildly man-shy. They'd not seen many humans and the few they had seen here they'd not learned to trust. Consequently, the dog had to do the biggest part of the penning. June's biddable. I can flank her by inches. All I needed to do was work this pen just like Luke and I worked the Maltese at Hafod Bridge. Be delicate, move them forward by inches. Let the sheep start trusting nothing is going to hurt them as they walk into the pen. Nothing will hurt them once they're inside it.

Lose no points at the pen or single and June and Donald will compete in the World Trials semifinals.

Maybe in my heart of hearts I knew that. Maybe that's why I lost it.

Visions are not created equal.

I tried a strategy that had failed for fifty handlers I'd seen over the pre-

LUKE, JUNE, AND DONALD AT THE END OF THE DAY

vious two days. I decided to put pressure on the sheep, waggle my cane at them, and then, like good little sheepies, they'd go into the pen.

Writing this months afterward, I can still picture that reluctant ewe as her wishy-washy pals walked into the pen and she slipped past. Boy, was she triumphant! And after she ran around the pen she ran around the pen and ran around the pen . . . Three times June and I penned four sheep. Four out of five is insufficient.

That first miss killed our semifinals chances, but we'd had a good run to this point and the judges let us continue a while longer before they called us off.

June was entirely whipped. She'd given absolutely everything she had to give and a bit more. She'd been beautiful.

There was a flapdoodle as we came off but I paid no mind until a steward produced Luke: "Is this your dog?"

When Luke thought June and I were in trouble, he'd bitten through his string lead to come help. A noncompeting sheepdog on the trial course is a disaster. DQ for its owner, and how can you apologize to the handler whose run you've ruined?

Fortunately, Luke didn't make his move until I'd finished and before the next handler began. Thank you, Lord.

I picked a pub where my grubby muddy clothes wouldn't excite comment, downed a pint, and got directions to the Llandeilo vet.

The vet was on the same square where we'd marched several lifetimes ago. Cars zipped through it now. I had no leash for Luke so I walked the Mister and Missus through traffic on a "get behind" (the sheepdogger's "heel").

The vet had been at the trial yesterday and asked which field we'd run on and how we'd done.

He set mud-pie Luke on a table. "Your dogs are well mannered, aren't they."

The vet took longer with Luke than with June. He frowned. He checked again. He said Luke had a heart murmur but he'd sign the certificate so I could fly him home.

AFTER I GOT HOME my vet examined Luke. Luke hates that slippery stainless steel examining table and fights back. Stressed, Luke's heart murmur was four on a scale of four. Luke's mitral valves weren't closing completely. My vet speculated that Luke's Lyme disease, contracted before I bought him, had caused the damage.

Sheepdog trials are terrific stress. More stress than my disapproval at his misbehavior, more stress than the lightless, deafening belly of an airliner, more than twenty-three hours to Texas in a car.

I recalled that Luke sometimes quit for no reason. I remembered how Luke quit at Gettysburg on the wrong side of that wall. Not enough blood, not enough oxygen to his brain; Luke worked until he ran out of heart.

I'd thought we had a training problem, some glitch in his personality.

Luke isn't the only blockhead in the pack.

Only a Dog

YOU DIDN'T KNOW how much you cared. Hell, she was only a dog. Nothing special. A Heinzy — 57 varieties. Just a mutt.

But she . . .

Six months after your dog died you still can't talk about her. You turn your face away, embarrassed by your tears.

Only a dog.

On a particularly bleak morning Anne told me, "I wake up and Zippy's gone and I wish I was dead too."

"Only a dog": that stupid heartless diminutive came straight from the Torah, the New Testament, and the Koran.

Why did the ancient Semites seek to disrupt that profound ancient connection between man and dog?

In legends of other native peoples, the dog is a benign and helpful creature — sometimes he's God's companion, sometimes he guards the underworld. Maria Leach's wonderful *God Has a Dog* names seventy native gods who had or used a dog.

Early nomadic Semitic peoples needed dogs for hunting, watchdogs, war, and to defend their all-important flocks. Torah commentaries count Abraham's sheep-guarding dogs among his wealth.

But Semitic writers never *once* praise the dog's virtues. The dog's fidelity and courage go unremarked. He is absent from the twenty-third psalm, and at Christ's nativity when terrifying angels brighten the night sky the shepherds' dogs don't bark.

I tuned into an evangelical radio broadcast whose preacher instructed children, "Sure you like old Spot and you must be kind to him, but remember, children, you have a soul and old Spot doesn't."

This doctrine troubles some devout Christians who hope to see their dog in an afterlife and, scripture to the contrary, presume they will.

Some trust that since theirs is a loving God He will slip their pets past Peter. More consistent Christians assume they will be so busy worshipping God in the afterlife they won't miss their dogs; that their love for Spot is merely an earthly love, no more precious than their affection for their Chevy Impala.

Early Semites worshiped gods of fertility and gods of war: Dagon and Hadad, and Baal, "the rider on the clouds." Often cruel, these gods required propitiation, but you could do business with them.

These capricious, somewhat manipulable gods might make a barren wife fertile, bring rain, or deflect an enemy's spear thrust; but these gods never shared with human worshippers their god-attributes, neither their power, nor their all-knowingness, nor their ability to live forever.

Aspiring to a god's powers was a bad idea. (See: Icarus.)

Belly full, protected by the watchful dog lying beside him, man began to dream of the impossible. We can trace the painfully slow, irresistible progress of this dream through the thirteen centuries of the Old Testament's creation.

Although they hedged their bets with Dagon, Baal, and the odd golden calf, some Semites began to dream of a single god. One can read the Pentateuch as the history of how Jews became monotheists. They swapped out a host of familiar, approachable gods with one remote, powerful, all-knowing, loving but extremely cranky Deity.

Why did God love a species that often denied Him, defied Him, and sometimes ranked Him second after that golden calf?

God loved weak, sinful, forgetful, rebellious man for one reason: "And God said: Let us make man in our image, after our likeness: and let them have dominion over the fish of the sea, over the fowl of the air, and over the cattle, and over all the earth."

That brilliant link made monotheism possible — just as there is one man, so there is one God. The worshipper is commanded to become "like" God (*imitatio Dei*). And surely, if we are "like" God, can't we share some of His attributes, even His immortality?

Emphatically, God did not make dog in His own image. Monotheism asserted an extreme human singularity that has engaged philosophers ever since: "Man, the featherless biped," "Man, the rational animal," "Homo

Faber," "Man, the animal that makes promises"... Our determination to distance ourselves from other animals — indeed from nature itself — has powered eco-catastrophes that endanger life on earth.

When God made man in His own image and gave him dominion over all other creatures, He simultaneously banished the dog from his special place at man's side.

The betrayal of dog by man, the "lost dog" story, is one of our oldest, most poignant tales. When Odysseus returns home after years of wandering, no creature recognizes him except his dying dog. "Infested with ticks, half dead from neglect, here lay the hound, old Argos. But the moment he sensed Odysseus standing by, he thumped his tail, muzzling low, and his ears dropped, though he had no strength to drag himself an inch toward his master."

Gelert was the favorite hound of the Welsh prince Llywelyn ab Iowerth. One day, Prince Llywelyn noticed that Gelert had abandoned the hunt. When the prince got home, the bloody Gelert greeted his master exuberantly, but the prince's infant son wasn't in his crib and blood splattered the nursery walls. The enraged prince promptly slew Gelert. Moments later he discovered his unharmed son, next to the corpse of the wolf Gelert had killed protecting the child.

There are at least thirty recorded versions of the Gelert story, the earliest before the Christian era.

"Lost dog" is paradigmatic; retold so many times in modern literature it seems the only dog story we need to tell: *White Fang, Lassie Come Home, The Incredible Journey, The Plague Dogs,* my own *Nop's Trials* — all stories of sundering and loss.

In Raymond Carver's "Jerry and Molly and Sam," an overwhelmed husband abandons the family dog beside the road: "He saw his whole life a ruin from here on. If he lived another fifty years — hardly likely — he felt he'd never get over it, abandoning the dog.... A man who would get rid of a little dog wasn't worth a damn. That kind of man would do anything, would stop at nothing."

We rewrite and reread this predictable, profoundly satisfying story although in each recounting, humans are cruel betrayers and dogs are our moral superiors.

The story satisfies because it is true. Because we betrayed the dog.

Our old partner, the animal who ensured our survival, who slipped into our genetic code like the missing piece of a jigsaw puzzle, became "only" a dog, no more privileged than hogs or cattle or sheep. We needed to spurn him because the dog threatened the dreams his watchfulness had made possible.

Freed by dog to dream of God, freed to yearn for a god's attributes, to escape the tragedy of human mortality, man gave up his dog for the greatest vision man has ever had.

Yet the dog remains eager — pathetically eager — to renew that hundred-thousand-year-old genetic partnership from which he has been forever banished: Lost Dog.

Man didn't abandon his dog cheaply. He didn't sell him for a mere thirty pieces of silver. Man asked the greatest reward any creature ever asked of his God: Immortality.

We lost our dog to live forever.

Your Dog

I WISH I COULD MEET your dog. I hope these stories remind you of him. I hope reading about Luke and June helps you see your dog a little better.

Ralph Pulfer was a sheepdog genius: his life was dogs. In fifty years, he won hundreds of trials. I once saw Ralph handle a young dog through a trial though the dog had never been taught commands. Ralph got him around the course using the dog's name, intoning "Tweed" so variously, that name was adequate dog grammar and vocabulary.

Not long before Ralph died, a handler asked him, "Ralph, how much do you understand about these dogs?"

Ralph didn't answer, but he wasn't much of a talker so somebody else picked up the conversation while Ralph went off to his RV.

Maybe an hour later, Ralph came back where the handlers were still gossiping.

Without preamble, Ralph interrupted: "I figure I understand about fifteen percent."

I'm not the handler Ralph was, but we have this in common: the gap between what we understand and what we wish to understand draws us on.

Some dog owners with mannerly dogs don't really "train" their dogs; they just know what a mannerly dog should do and "expect" their dog to do it.

On the other hand, I've known owners deeply invested in their dog's inabilities. Some believed their ill-trained dog was proof positive of their personal kindliness, patience, and all-forgivingness. Some fatheads chuckled condescendingly at their dogs' failures. Others identified with a badly behaved aggressive pooch. Their dog served as their outlaw doppelganger.

What do you want from your dog?

Can you invite people to your home? Can you take your dog anywhere? Can you leave him alone at home?

Or do you seek the same clear-eyed, intimate dance with your dog I am trying to learn? That doesn't come easy or cheap. Wanna take a chance?

Can you commit yourself — as surely and thoroughly as your dog will?

These decisions aren't up to your dog; they're up to you. No dog has ever signed up for training lessons or entered a sheepdog trial. Pet dog trainer Vivian Bregman's bright red T-shirt reads, "You are the Trainer. I am the Instructor." *You* are the dog trainer. And, as Ms. Greenlief asks, "Are you training your dog, or is your dog training you?"

Are you a little embarrassed to be asking for help — with a mere dog? Perhaps you've got an advanced degree, perhaps you manage gazillions of dollars, maybe you have the president's private e-mail addy. Why should you upset your schedule to train a mere dog?

Because that's the only way to do it. Despite President Obama's power to have anyone do pretty much anything, Bo, the White House dog, is ill-trained.

Like you, if the president of the United States wants a well-trained dog, he must train it.

Despite a quarter century of experience, I regularly sign up for training clinics and private coaching. Unless your dog is too old to learn — or you are — you should do the same.

At a minimum you'll have a dog that enriches your life, instead of troubling it. Pursue training far enough, deep enough, and profound changes occur.

Okay, you'll give it a go. But who to believe in an acrimonious profession whose different schools regularly denounce their competitors as abusers, ineffectuals, and/or frauds?

For a lucky few, the answer is easy. If you are a novice working dog trainer you must use the methods successful handlers use. Working dog trainers can't do their job nor win ribbons and prize money if their training is ineffectual or abusive. You can safely assume that your dog culture's methods work just fine, whatever their theoretical inadequacies.

Do not, for the sake of "correct" philosophy or "correct" tools, ignore the hard-earned wisdom of those with years of more complex human/dog conversations than you can presently articulate. When seeking a trainer, "monkey see, monkey do" is excellent advice.

I once had a long, ultimately fruitless argument with a prominent e-collar trainer who offered to train my sheepdogs with his e-collar, although the man knew nothing about sheep or stockwork and had never previously trained a sheepdog nor seen one trained. Despite his thoroughgoing ignorance of the work, he proposed to use his e-collar on Luke and June. He thought he was being generous. His time was so valuable. I thought he was dumber than your average bear.

If you are training for agility or flyball and your mentor trains with a clicker and treats, purchase a clicker and a treat bag. If you're training retrievers, bird dogs, or coon dogs, buy an e-collar. If you intend to achieve top honors in AKC obedience, find a traditional mentor and study Bill Koehler and the Volhards.

If, like most dog owners, you don't want a working dog but do want a mannerly family pet, choosing an instructor and a method is iffier. Whatever your choice there are no panaceas: you (that's YOU I'm talking to!) must find the time and do the work to train your dog.

Every trainer I spoke to, though advocating methods as contradictory as Koehler and pharmacological behaviorism, agreed on four basic principles. They are *magic* principles, and so important that training may not help dogs living without them, while some dogs living with them may require little formal training.

Magic principle #1: Don't be nuts! Functional human families rear healthy children, pay their bills, work hard for the common good, and, not incidentally, own mannerly dogs. Dogs are pack animals and take their cues from the pack. Bad pack = bad dog. No dog can cure a dysfunctional family, but dysfunctional families have destroyed more dogs than I want to think about.

Magic principle #2: Puppies are baby dogs. They poop on the floor for the same reason undiapered babies would poop on the floor: because they haven't control over their bowels.

Your puppy is, like that baby, a pack animal, and your family is your puppy's pack. He needs to be played with, walked, talked to, and caressed. He needs to know the household's rules. Relax the rules from time to time, let the pup jump on the couch or beg at the table or jump up on visitors, and the rules won't be pack rules anymore: they'll become futile nagging.

Unsocialized or poorly socialized pups become fearful, aggressive, or unpredictable adults. Dogs with a weak bond with their human pack are more difficult to train and often end up on the shelter's death row.

Your pup won't learn much about life or human expectations if he spends endless lonely days on a chain, in a kennel, or in a fenced yard. You wouldn't keep your child in a bubble until he was an adult and expect him to function in the world, but many owners do exactly that with their dogs. Like us, dogs learn from experience.

Training can bring your dog out of the bubble safely into the world where both of you can learn from your subsequent shared experience.

You'll be better for it.

If both you and your spouse work and the kids are in school and after-school soccer practice or dance class or Bible class or . . . and there's nobody home to socialize a puppy, please don't get a puppy. You're not a cruel person.

Magic principle #3: Exercise your dog. A fenced backyard is a fence around a backyard: a fence is NOT exercise. Yes, off-lead exercise is better — dogs easily run five miles for the one you walk and my dogs rarely wear a lead. But I live on a remote mountain farm where off-lead exercise is easy. Flexi-leads are dangerous for dogs and humans and snout loops (sorry, "head halters") are abusive, but if you can't exercise your dog without them, clip on. Perfect is and always has been the enemy of good.

Tired dogs, even poorly trained tired dogs, are mannerly dogs. As Behesha Doan says, "The first thing the dog does every morning is ask, 'What's different today?'" And by God, your dog will have his answer. He is bursting with energy and if you don't help him express that energy, he'll release it in ways you won't like. Your dog zooming around the dog park is good fun; that same dog zooming around your kitchen is broken crockery.

What's the bare minimum? Two fifteen-minute walks every single day, rain or shine, snow or fog. Go ahead, clip the leash to the dog's collar and carry an umbrella. The walk'll be good for you too — get a little oxygen in your brain.

You're too busy? Too busy for two fifteen-minute walks? Well then, re-arrange your life so you're not too busy. You need a sheepdog trainer to tell you that?

Magic principle #4: Give your dog a job. Some people say (and may be-lieve) that what they want from their dog is unconditional love. I think they're kidding themselves and if they got unconditional love they'd be bored witless. Only sickos and celebs crave adoration.

I distrust one-way relationships. I don't want all the power, I cannot pos-sibly be right all the time. Sometimes my sheepdog knows more than I do.

Your dog can only be right if, like Luke and June, your dog has a job. Dropping the tennis ball into your hand after he's chased it, a proper sit be-fore you put down his dinner bowl, steady to wing and shot, a good listener, a clean runner — give your dog a chance to do a shared task correctly and your relationship will deepen fast.

So: socialize, exercise, give your dog a job, and, oh yeah — don't be nuts. There's no mystery, no daunting skills required, and every trainer I know will give the same advice I've just offered. Dog trainers sometimes talk themselves out of a job.

But, suppose you rescued your dog from the Bite-A-Wee-Dog Shelter, he was poorly socialized, and living with your new family pet is less fun than the Gotterdammerung. Or maybe you, like me, want a dog who'll test your limits as you test his. Maybe you want a dog who asks more than you think you have to offer.

Pal, then you need a trainer.

Which trainer would I recommend? That's easy too: I'd recommend the trainer who shares my goals. You should do likewise.

Traditionalists Tony Ancheta, Behesha Doan, and Wendy Volhard train for "obedience," which can be measured at formal obedience trials. Training success is measured objectively by performance and successes in the obedience ring. Their explicit goal is real-world off-lead reliability in the presence of real-world distractions.

Pat Miller and Nicholas Dodman believe almost all corrections are cruel, and their goals are less specific. They want to keep the dog in the home rather than see it relinquished to the animal shelter. They use training, management, and pharmaceuticals to achieve that goal. Tethers and snout loops can deter the strongest dogs from jumping on guests or towing their frail owner.

Positive trainers often advise those seeking a trainer to "inquire about the trainer's philosophy." Positive trainers have, in behaviorism, a coherent philosophy, while most traditionalists shrug and offer some variant of "whatever works." Owners with an intellectual bent may find positive methods appealing. Ditto for those who like to believe their training methods are "scientific."

Positive training can achieve modest goals and perhaps a bit more. Pat Miller's Lucy could easily earn her CD. Positive training does take longer than traditional training, and, in the end, dog management is no timesaver. It doesn't take long to train a dog to not jump up. If he must be restrained by tethering each time guests arrive, you will be tethering how often for how many visits for how many years?

But these inconveniences may not weigh as heavily on you as your wish to be and to be seen as a kind, caring, positive dog owner.

Dog tail-chasing, light- or shadow-chasing, and similar obsessive-compulsive behaviors are difficult to train away and pharmaceutical intervention may be the best remedy. Prozac-like drugs are expensive and may have undesirable side effects as they did for Luke. But if your dog is eating his own tail or biting insects that aren't there, side effects and cost may be irrelevant. Some traditional trainers deny separation anxiety exists. Dr. Dodman insists it exists and isn't rare. I think they're both right.

Although most trainers have stable dog packs, many pet owners have only one dog. Urban/suburban dogs can form temporary packs — same time every day at the dog park or doggy day care — but for many pets all their pack members are human and when the humans go out the door, the pack is *gone*. Add insufficient exercise and no training or shared work, and you've a recipe for a very anxious canine.

For such dogs, Prozac may be best.

Positive trainers like to say their method is less risky than traditional (correction-based) training, and I think they're right — remember how Luke's difficulty finding sheep he couldn't see was triggered by a single inappropriate, badly timed correction?

One day Shay McMullen's immature dog Lad was spotting sheep for novices. A novice's dog screwed up his outrun and the novice ran up the field bellowing at it. Lad — who was *not* being corrected — decided that the top end of the field, near sheep, was a dangerous place. It took several years for Lad to unlearn one powerful, incorrect, unintended lesson.

I've seen more than a few sheepdogs ruined, and, sadly, this often happens with the most promising, precocious young dogs. There's a learning window of opportunity between the onset of dog puberty and psychological maturity — the sheepdog learns quickest between, roughly, six months and two years old. But that quick-learning young dog isn't emotionally mature, and if pushed beyond his understanding of his pack and his world, a single over-the-top, angry correction can scar a dog for years if not for life.

Positive trainers also claim that positive methods don't inhibit the dog from offering new behaviors, whereas correction training shuts a dog down. That's gobbledygook.

I believe pet dogs can be brought to off-leash (though not off-collar) reliability fastest with an e-collar. Naive dogs respond quickly to the tool, and e-collars are not cruel *in the hands of an experienced trainer.* In an unskilled owner's hands — or in my hands for that matter — cruelty is an all too real possibility. Dog isn't doing what it ought? Crank the sucker up to nine — that'll get his attention! Recently I was walking dogs with an e-collar trainer and his students. When a pet owner's dog yelped, the trainer reproved, "It's too hot. Turn it down. The dog is vocalizing."

Marketing euphemisms pervade dog training. E-collars? Gentle Leaders? Positive Training? Vocalizing? Nope, that dog was yelping.

The e-collar-trained dogs I've seen were as happy with their lot as dogs trained by other traditional methods and were less confused than the dogs I saw in Pat Miller's novice class.

To the non-dog-savvy owner, the e-collar promises total remote control. Why do you think that's a good thing? Do you know as much about being a dog as your dog does? Dogs aren't robots. Good training, as Vicki Hearne observed, is a conversation. *Not* a goddamned monologue.

The sheer power of the shock collar is why it should be restricted to skilled trainers with experience, good timing, and dog sense. Yes, any tool can be abused, but the shock collar positively invites abuse. (Stanley

Milgram's psychological experiments on ordinary people's willingness to become torturers are pertinent here.) It is very easy for an angry civilian to turn a collar up to full power and hit that button again and again.

In 2005 I was asked to do a demo at the IACP conference, where many trainers' dogs wore e-collars. We were standing outdoors in the sunshine waiting for a lecture to start. Nice morning, light breeze, many, many mannerly dogs. Suddenly a dog shrieked. Its owner understood why: her dog's e-collar and another's were on the same frequency and someone was repeatedly shocking her dog. "Stop stimming! Please stop stimming!" the owner cried. Her dog bolted down the road, mindless and terrified. Yes, that particular problem is extremely rare. How often are you in a group of a hundred e-collared dogs? But too much control has a way of coming back to bite you.

If you rarely lose your temper with your dog and have access to a trainer/mentor as good as Behesha Doan, the e-collar can be a wonderful tool. I have used one and might use it again. But it scares the bejesus out of me.

While most traditional trainers use some of Bill Koehler's methods (especially the longe line), there aren't many "pure" Koehler trainers today. Most pet dog owners will not or cannot train one evening every week for thirteen weeks — however effective that training may be. While traditional trainers admire Koehler, most add treats, puppy tests, drive theory, ethology, and e-collars to the Koehler method.

"Off-leash reliability" is the traditional trainer's explicit goal, but that is more mantra than commonplace. During my tour of training facilities I met many well-trained dogs, but few were off lead. Many trainers are uncomfortable meeting off-lead or off-e-collar dogs. They argue that unknown off-lead dogs might attack their mannerly dogs, but they're professionals who, of all people, should be able to see trouble coming and prevent it. I know I can.

As ye train, so shall ye go. If you train with treats, you'll carry a treat bag whenever you walk your dog. If you train with an e-collar, choke collar, or prong collar, you'll be reluctant to remove your tool.

Your training method becomes your default. I train with voice corrections, and my country neighbor complains she sometimes hears me hollering two miles away.

In any case, no human has perfect control of any dog. I may lose my voice, head halters can break, treats may be unenticing, the e-collar's batteries may fail.

Though each trainer believes his or her method is best, I don't think it matters which method the pet owner adopts so long as that owner finds a capable mentor and sticks with the training. Eventually you will learn to see your dog and when that happens the richness of your and your dog's lives will tell you what to do next.

Neither Luke nor June was ever trained to "heel" nor "sit" nor "stand for examination." They have never retrieved a ball or dumbbell. They rarely play with each other and never play with other dogs. Yet they would be mannerly in any human environment. Not because they were "trained" for good manners, but because they were properly socialized, exercised daily, and have a job — stock work. Mannerliness is a by-product of that training.

SIMILARLY, your dog isn't more mannerly because he can heel and sit and fetch. It is the training itself — the work of training, the commitment, the necessary bonding of human and dog that training promotes — that creates a mannerly dog. And, not incidentally, a wiser, richer human being.

As Jack Volhard says, "Training builds the integrity of your relationship with your dog."

Have the highest expectations, do the work, and your dog can walk at your side anywhere on earth. He'll become the dog you've empowered to change your life. As Luke and June have changed mine.

First Friends

THE MORNING AFTER June and I didn't qualify for the semifinals of the World Sheepdog Trials was cool and foggy.

I didn't attend the semifinals. The dogs and I hiked across sand dunes toward the distant beach. Other dog-walkers appeared and disappeared in the fog but none came near. It was a morning for mistakes, for getting turned around and walking miles and miles and miles through the sand.

If visions are not created equal, I suppose mine had been one of the better ones.

The Mister and Missus explored. The tide was out and shorebirds patrolled and pecked in the dark sand where the ocean had been.

I perched on the wreck of a plastic bucket that had floated from somewhere else. Shreds of plastic twine entangled driftwood. Bleached, scuffed plastic somethings were half buried in the sand. A gull's caw was sweeter and lonelier than the ravens' cry back home.

The leaves would be turning on our north slopes, first the walnuts, then the gold oaks and the shocking red maples.

Soon it would frost and wood smoke would curl from our chimney.

On this faraway shore, Luke and June rolled in the sand. They shook themselves and rolled again. Luke grinned. June's tongue lolled.

After a time, June came and lay beside me. Luke was busy on a scent trail but when he noticed that we were still, he returned and flopped down on my other side. June licked her paws.

Waves hissed against the wide Atlantic beach.

Puzzled, Luke frowned and thumped his tail tentatively. When that drew no response, he got up, shook himself, and shouldered into a sand roll. He writhed. Four furry feet waved in the air. My dog grinned like a fool.

"Come on, Boss," Luke said. "Wave your feet! Give us a roll!"

Would that I could.

The Double Lift

UNDAY WAS CLEAR; no fog and the light was incandescent. The dogs and I drove to Llandielo for the finals of the World Sheepdog Trials. At important trials, the ultimate competition is the "double lift," and the World Trials would be no exception. The double lift is the most difficult test of a sheepdog. We ask the dogs to do more than they can and those that manage are asked to do the nearly impossible.

Dinefwr Park had dried out. Luke, June, and I were parked by pleasant volunteers wearing vests with "Steward" on the front and "Sorry for the Delay" on the back.

A zillion cars were pouring in and more concessions and diversions had appeared. The four-hundred-seat restaurant would be open until five o'clock. Trick riders, search and rescue teams, and celebrity chefs did demos. Hooded raptors perched silently waiting for their show.

I left the dogs in the car and beelined to the grandstand. My back and knees couldn't tolerate one more day on my feet.

My new friend, the Hafod Bridge trial secretary, cried, "Ah, Donald. I have a crook for you. When I thought you'd be here I went to the riverbank and cut it." It was a thick stem of crook wood, with a branch at the top where my thumb could rest. I thanked him and asked if I could buy a grandstand pass.

"Oh, no. No," he said cheerfully. "Sold out weeks ago. Go 'round up the hill. You'll see better from there anyway."

Discouraged, I went for coffee instead. Most mornings I'd got on the road so early I hadn't used the "breakfast" part of my B&B, and today had been no exception.

When I came back to the grandstand my Welsh friend hissed, "Donald, you don't have a ticket?"

"No."

"Here then. But don't tell anyone I got it for you."

The Reverend Canon W. Roger Hughes, dean of Llangadog/Llandielo, would lead the morning worship service. Roger loves sheepdogs and had come to all the trials. Usually Roger was in waterproofs and wellies but it was black cassock today.

This morning, he took the mic to announce that the service would be held in front of the Tesco Pavilion where those who might wish to come could and those who didn't wish to come probably needed to.

He noted that loudspeakers would carry the service throughout the grounds and those who needed to couldn't escape it anyway.

A hundred attended the service.

"Welcome! Croeso cynnes," the dean began.

This was Christianity with a crook. Our opening hymn was "Christ our Shepherd, all souls calling . . . ," and Tony Iley, whose lovely memoir *Sheepdogs at Work* went through four editions, read the gospel.

In his homily, Roger Hughes described the lost sheep in expert detail: "Everyone thinks of that sheep as a fluffy little lamb but she's not. She's been in the briars and the thickets, she hasn't been shorn, and she's probably got manure tags. She's smelly and unpleasant. Quite possibly the flock has cast her out, yet Christ the Shepherd seeks her — whether she wants Him to or not . . ."

We sang the twenty-third psalm and an American, John Seraphine, prayed: "Lord, we thank you for our dogs — your simple gift to us. Open us to what they teach.

"We thank you for the grateful exuberance of our dogs. We thank you for the way they bound across the hills, splash in the waters, chew on sticks, and roll in the dewy grass. Teach us, every day, to say our own 'thank you' with every fiber of our being, for the wondrous works of your creation.

"We thank you, Lord, for the honest, direct loyalty of our dogs. We thank you for the wag of their tails and the offer of a cuddle for friend and stranger alike, the way they make people from twenty-two nations into our neighbors, the way they regard not body type, color of hair, or color of skin. We thank you for the easy way they forgive faults — the way they love us, not because we can love back, but because of our need for love. Teach us, every day, to open our hands and hearts to friend and foreigner, and to be reborn to the power of free and fearless compassion.

"We thank you Lord for the ageless wisdom of our dogs, who know things and do things that no book or computer chip can contain. Teach us, every day, to cherish what our neighbors know and what they can do. Help us to treasure the skills and arts of shepherds and farmers, cooks and cleaners and clerks, painters of landscapes and painters of schoolhouse walls. Help us to notice . . . help us appreciate . . . help us say 'thank you,' with our smiles and with our words, for the ageless wisdom of our neighbors that we depend on for our very lives.

"We thank you, Lord, for the way our dogs breathe deeply in and sigh deeply out before they settle and sleep. Teach us to live each moment of life as fully as they do and then to rid ourselves of the worries of the world as we commend to you our spirits. Teach us the deep mystery of peaceful sleep and peaceful death — to trust that the new dawn will come tomorrow, yet another of your surprising, simple gifts.

"We thank you Lord for our shepherding dogs who can't stand to lose track of the wayward lamb. We are your lambs, O Lord, and oh so often lost. Teach us, every day, to remember your fanatical eagerness to gather us back to your flock and fold, even as we pray the prayer your Shepherd Son has taught us to pray:

"Our Father . . ."

AFTER THE SERVICE, I climbed into the grandstand. The seats were too small and I squeezed in between the old hunchbacked shepherd (no danger of his falling asleep today) and David Rees. I intended to visit Barbara Carpenter on my way home and needed her phone number. As David and I gossiped, the Reverend Canon Hughes appeared in front of the grandstand, put his hands on his hips, and thundered, "You know David Rees, when I was talking about the lost sheep, I was talking about YOU!"

David grinned. "I'm no the lost sheep. I'm the black sheep!"

We and the Reverend Canon laughed.

I'd dreamed of this day for years: getting into the semifinals and if it pleased God through to the finals. I'd trained for that vision, trialed for it, driven thousands of miles, spent Lord Knows How Much, prayed, and invoked Rachael's long-distance June-magic. We live and die for our visions.

At the double lift, the handler must send his dog (today to the right) on a blind (five-hundred-yard) outrun to find, lift, and fetch ten sheep to a stake just inside the fetch panels.

Then the handler gives his dog the "look back" command, and the fun begins. The dog has worked hard gathering and fetching ten sheep and now his handler tells him: "Not these sheep; some other sheep."

Faith, as St. Paul reminds us, is valuing the unseen over the seen.

For the sheepdog this is a profound conceptual problem: abandoning gathered sheep is not in sheepdog genetics. The sheepdog must have absolute faith in his handler to quit the sheep-in-the-hand for sheep that might-be-out-there-somewhere although he cannot see them.

While flocklet #1 stands around or drifts or grazes, the Faithful Sheepdog runs out five hundred yards for flocklet #2. When he finds them he fetches #2 (in a straight line, naturally) through the fetch panels to combine with #1.

Okay. The drive and crossdrive are per usual, except your dog has twenty sheep to squeeze through the panels instead of five. Crowded at the opening, nervous ewes often slip around instead of through.

The dog gets your enlarged flock through the crossdrive panels and into the hundred-foot shedding ring which today becomes the circle of the blessed and the damned.

Five of your sheep wear bright red collars. They've been randomly collared and may never have grazed together.

Or they may have . . . Sheep do bond — ewe with lamb, twin lamb with her sister — and some pals are inseparable. Sometimes, at the home farm a today-collared and a today-uncollared ewe invariably graze together, walk side by side, drink water side by sider, and do the amiable things bonded sheep do together.

Without knowing their ovine biographies the handler and dog must shed the five collared sheep from the fifteen uncollared, inside the shedding ring. Neither handler nor dog can touch them.

It's called the "international shed." You're on one side of the sheep, your dog's on the other. Using the dog as a faux gate, you urge uncollared sheep — four, five, or six — to drift away from the flock. These sheep will serve as the "draw," the magnet attracting sheep shed later.

Then you amble around until your chosen uncollared sheep come into the invisible gateway — before you open the (dog) gate and one, two, or three more ewes trot off to join the draw.

Since any single uncollared sheep will be nervous and reluctant to leave the safety of the collared, you ought not winnow down to one uncollared and five collared ewes.

If any collared sheep gets through your dog gate to join the uncollared sheep (the draw) you must bring every one back and start over.

After you sort them into collared and uncollared, you pen the five collared ewes. That's it. All done. From the moment your dog begins its outrun, you have thirty minutes. Often the international shed takes half that time.

An American teammate turned in her seat and murmured, "I really wanted to be out there today, but right now, I'm really glad I'm not."

Not me.

On the green, green field, in Vermeer light, John Wood (English) walked to the post with Moe at his side.

Moe, Spot, Tweed, Rock, Cap, Rob, Roy, Floss, Bill, Jim, Mirk, Recca, Sammie, Nell, Eira, and Joe. The best sheepdogs in the world are working-class blokes who'd stand you a pint after the day's work.

There were seven Welsh finalists, five other Brits, a Norwegian woman with a gyp everybody admired, a New Zealander (he'd been in Britain three months practicing), a Dane, and a Dutchman. No Americans made the cut. Alasdair MacRae and Tommy Wilson got through to the semifinals, but Alasdair drew bad sheep and Tommy was singling when he was caught by the standard.

Today, four judges pointed faults: Rushed lift? Bad line on the second fetch? Collared sheep step out of the shedding ring? Dog out of contact?

Fifteen hundred knowledgeable spectators packed the grandstands. When Kevin Evans and Spot sorted their final uncollared ewes and Kevin turned away, Spot thought it'd be fun to reunite the sorted ewes with the unsorted. At the spectators' gasp, Kevin spun back. "SPOT!!!!"

I went to check on my dogs, and paused at the Countryside Alliance booth. The Alliance was formed when Prime Minister Tony Blair pushed through a law prohibiting foxhunting.

Oscar Wilde famously called foxhunting "the unspeakable in pursuit of the inedible." It is also brilliant, beautiful, and insanely dangerous.

Foxhunting is a mainstay of rural British traditions and economy and four hundred thousand country folk traveled to London to protest the ban.

The hunts found ways around the law. Foxhunting is more popular than ever and the Tories have promised to repeal the ban should they return to power.

Llandielo Hunt foxhounds were at the World Trials to be sponsored and for fifteen pounds I sponsored fuzzy-faced Bouncer. The master promised to send me a photo of my foxhound.

On the trial field, Richard Millichap and Cap were in trouble. The draw (uncollareds) had drifted over a rise where the sole remaining uncollared ewe couldn't see them. Richard's magnet had gone dead. Worse, Richard had shed that single ewe once and she'd gotten fifty yards away before galloping back to the collared ewes, leaping over Cap in the process. That uncollared ewe was scared and stubborn; she knew exactly what Richard meant to do and wanted no part of it.

Ten minutes remaining. What had been a fine run was toast. That uncollared ewe clung to the collared sheep closer than a chastity belt. Richard worked quietly and Cap did as bid for eight of those ten minutes when, suddenly, as if by magic, that single popped out of the others and wandered up the hill. She stopped dead, staring at thousands of humans. "You've all come here just to admire little old me?" Celebrity sheep.

Richard and Cap penned to terrific applause.

No, they didn't win. Aled Owen and Roy took home the solid gold shepherd's whistle, the enormous trophy, and the check for three thousand pounds, but Richard and Cap didn't exactly lose either.

The hunchbacked shepherd shook his head and sighed. On the field, the next sheepdog was outrunning, swift and soft as light. The old herd turned to me. His eyes were clear as a boy's. "They are brilliant, aren't they?" he said. "Absolutely brilliant. The dogs."

Acknowledgments

My thanks to:
Tony Ancheta: www.koehlerdogtraining.com
Behesha Doan: www.extremek-9.com
Dr. Nicholas Dodman: www.thepetdocs.com
Pat Miller: www.peaceablepaws.com
Jack and Wendy Volhard: www.volhard.com

And to the photographers who gave permission to use their photographs:
June: Shay McMullen
Luke: Richard Robinson
Mr. Grumpy (author photo): Maureen Robinson
Mr. and Mrs. Dog by Mr. Grumpy himself
World Trials photographs by Stacey Scott

Nickolass Tinbergen's account of his friendship with Konrad Lorenz is from his Nobel Foundation autobiography.

The Reverend John Seraphine's sermon and the Volhards' test are used by permission.

Also by Donald McCaig